An Ideal
Farm Husband

Reviews

Reviews for *How To Be A Perfect Farm Wife*

"I laughed out loud several times ... Being a farmer's wife herself, the author knows only too well the many hardships of farming. But this book brings a sense of energy and perspective to the subject, which is refreshing and ultimately uplifting." Ann Fitzgerald, *Irish Independent*

"As an investment banker turned farmer's wife, this is funny, educational, really interesting and exactly what I need. A joy to read." Aideen Fleming

"The book will have a valued place among other social commentaries that deal with the contingencies of Irish farming life. It will also fulfil the role of an old friend, waiting quietly until she is needed for advice and reassurance, or is simply sought out for the pleasure of her company." Jonathan Bell, *Farming Life*

"It is not simply a delightful page-turner, nor is it only for those with a farming background. Despite the tongue-in-cheek title and chapter headings that suggest a light-hearted read, the book is eminently informative and revealing about the position of women in Irish society. As such, it should appeal to anyone with an interest in social history." Ciara Meehan, Head of History, University of Hertfordshire

Reviews for *Would You Marry A Farmer?*

"Lorna's observations on the daily life of the farmer's wife had me laughing out loud in recognition ... written with great warmth and affection." *Horse and Countryside*

"She writes with authority and from experience and no doubt her sense of humour, much in evidence throughout the book, has enabled her to cope with the ups and downs of marrying a farmer." Teagasc, *Today's Farm Magazine*

An Ideal Farm Husband

Lorna Sixsmith

Write on Track Press
An Ideal Farm Husband
Lorna Sixsmith

The images for bullets © Bigstock (wellie, bioraven; teapot, ratkom) Shutterstock (ring, Main1)

Published in Ireland by Write on Track
ISBN: 978-1537636290

To Brian, Will and Kate

ABOUT THE AUTHOR

Lorna Sixsmith was reared on a dairy and beef farm in Co. Laois, the eldest of three children. Allergic to dairy products, grass pollens, straw and some animals, the chances of becoming the perfect farmer were certainly slim. Lorna worked as a teacher in Wiltshire, England while her husband, Brian James, worked as a scientist. They returned to Ireland in 2002 when their eldest child was three weeks old to take over the family farm. They now live there with their children Will and Kate, their two dogs Sam and Lou, numerous farm cats and 120 cows.

Lorna divides her year into three parts: the calving season February–April; her writing season April–August, and September–January is when she markets and sells her books, as well as catching up on reading novels. She also trains businesses how to use social media and provides a copy writing service. Tea is her favourite tipple as long as it comes with chocolate or home-made cake.

Lorna has had short stories published in two anthologies: *Around the Farm Gate* (2015), edited by PJ Cunningham and *Then There Was Light* (2016), edited by PJ Cunningham and Joe Kearney. *An Ideal Farm Husband* is the third of her non-fiction books, preceded by *Would You Marry A Farmer?* and *How To Be A Perfect Farm Wife*.

ACKNOWLEDGEMENTS

Writing a non-fiction book like this means undertaking research and once again, farmers helped out by answering questions about their own farm lives and experiences. I'd like to thank Sarah Brandt, Linda & George Cliffe, Sarah Jane Drummond, Fiona Graham, William Healy, Fiona Lake, Elissa and Phillip Miller, Joe and Ruby Sixsmith and the many others who answered queries on my Facebook page or within groups on Facebook. The Irish News Archive makes it relatively easy to find relevant newspaper articles and advertisements so it's a great resource. Thanks also to women I've met who work in agriculture in various ways: Martina Calvey, Mary Carey Ryan, Joan Collins, Suzanna Crampton, Sheila Crowley, Catherina Currane, Ann Doran, Catherine Guest, Margaret Hoctor, Jane Kavanagh, Patricia Kelliher, Aisling Molloy, Eileen Moynihan, Ann Stenning and Leonie Vella.

I've been lucky enough to get to know many authors and avid readers. The staff in Castlecomer Library, especially Mary Morrissey, and those in Carlow Library have been most helpful. It's been fun writing with others in the Carlow Writers Group led by John McKenna. I've met many wonderful writers through the Wexford Literary Festival and I'd like to give a few a special thank you: Caroline Busher, Carmel Harrington and Cat Hogan. I'd like to thank all the bookshop and gift shop owners that stock my books, every journalist that has interviewed me and every book blogger who reviewed my books. To you, the reader, thank you and I hope you enjoy the read.

It's wonderful to have made friends among other business women and I don't see them often enough. However, whenever we do meet up, we always make up for it by talking nonstop. Thank you for friendship, chat and advice: Sarah Byrne, Aideen Fleming, Madeleine Forrest, Una Halpin, Miriam Lloyd, Bianka McDonagh, Ciara Meehan, Sian Phillips, Dee Sewell, Paula Sheridan, Tara Sparling, Bernie Tracey, Jojanneke van den Bosch, Elizabeth Walsh, Lisa Walsh McGee, Amanda Webb and Ruth Wildgust.

Self-publishing is a fun journey and I love the challenges of writing, producing, marketing and selling my own books. There are a few people involved in the process who make it a lot easier. Tony and Mark at Naas Printing are extremely helpful and professional. I'd like to thank Derry Dillon for his wonderful illustrations and cover design, interpreting my instructions for each illustration so well. Sally Vince, my editor, does a superb job of editing and formatting my books and I can't tell you how wonderful it feels to be able to send my manuscript off into her capable hands. It's great to be able to bounce ideas off someone else and as a result of Sally's mentoring I have a long list of writing projects to keep me busy for the next couple of years.

I'm delighted to be launching this book at the *Irish Independent* stand at the Ploughing Championships 2016 and would like to thank the staff of the *Irish Independent*, especially Arlene Regan, marketing manager, and Louise Hogan, *Farming Independent* editor, and Ann Fitzgerald for doing me the honour of launching my book.

To Brian, for not complaining when I share so much of our lives in yet another book and for reading my final draft late at night when you really needed some sleep; to Will, for your jokes and infectious laughter; to Kate, for your sharp wit and wonderful smile, thank you all for always looking on the bright side of life.

CONTENTS

What do those farmyard idioms mean?

Some might think that country people "go around the houses" when describing things, but in reality we have terms that hit the nail on the head. And as you might expect, they include farmyard animals. I've included some of those sayings throughout the book.

INTRODUCTION

If you were to ask men and women why they decided to farm, many will say they didn't want to do anything else. Most of us lucky enough to be brought up on a farm had a great upbringing, an almost idyllic childhood, and the chance to continue that with our own children is something many farmers look forward to. Some might say they had no choice; they were pressured to continue the farm and while a few may hanker to do something else, most can look back on a career in farming with satisfaction.

Why can't you just be a farmer – why the need to be Ideal Farm Husband? You see, it's still usually men who inherit; women tend to enter farming by falling in love with a farmer. While the majority of farm wives in previous generations came from farming backgrounds, many farm wives have little or no experience of farm life, which is why you need this book.

It has long been known by farmers that a wife is essential for the successful running of the farm and newspapers have emphasised this too. According to the *Nenagh Guardian* in 1965, a judge of a small farms competition commented that "all the good farms they had visited had three things in common, 'good grass, good cows and a good woman in the house'."[1] Many articles state that farmers are much more successful when their wives are involved in the running of the business[2] thereby

1

emphasising the power of good teamwork between you and your perfect farm wife. See, you need her to stick around but you also need to be able to reap the benefits of farming, ensuring your family has a harmonious and good quality of life.

Learning how to become an ideal farm spouse (male or female) takes preparation, hard work and some give and take too. My previous two books *Would You Marry A Farmer?* and *How To Be A Perfect Farm Wife* explored farming life from the female perspective, showing women how to prepare for life married to a farmer and how to enjoy it. But don't men need instruction in reaching perfection too, or perhaps more importantly, on recognising that they do so much that is good already? Somewhat following the structure of Shakespeare's *All The World's A Stage*, *An Ideal Farm Husband* shows you how to find the love of your life, persuade her to love you and the farm, have a wonderful wedding, reach your 50th anniversary and retire gracefully, all while running a farm successfully.

To all farm husbands (and farm wives), I hope *An Ideal Farm Husband* provides you with lots of laughs as well as tips, and maybe it will make you realise that you weren't too far off being almost ideal after all.

Lorna Sixsmith
Garrendenny, Crettyard, Co. Laois, Ireland.
September 2016

PART ONE

IS MARRYING A FARMER IDEAL?

A COCKTAIL OF HEROES

I'm sure many men think they would make an ideal farm husband. After all, their mothers seemed happy as long as they turned up for their meals and muttered a few words of appreciation as she rushed from A to B and C to D and back to A to start cooking all over again.

The first step is to recognise that a mother's love is usually unconditional. She has helped to form you into what you have become and you will always be the apple of her eye. A wife's love tends to be conditional, so you can't rest on your laurels. You need to know what is expected of an Ideal Farm Husband so you can strive to become one.

We'll start by examining what women in the past considered to be an ideal husband. You'll find out exactly what you should be doing to get it right and you might discover a few surprises along the way too.

According to the *Kilkenny People* on 22 October 1904, Miss Pauline Griffith decided her ideal husband would be:

> as handsome as Apollo, with the courage of Michael, the strength of Shadow, the subtlety of Machiavelli, the patriotism of Emmet, and have the patience of Job.[3] He should be able to eat anything set before him without grumbling; able to smile sweetly when he

finds his papers scattered all over the floor; and the baby blowing soap bubbles; good tempered when I point my pencils with his razor, and happy when I bring my mother and four sisters to live with me.

She concludes, quite rightly I think, by saying she has her doubts she will be able to secure such a man. Whatever about him staying in a good mood when she blunted his razor and messed up his newspaper, adding a mother-in-law and four sisters-in-law to the equation would definitely be pushing it. If the prospect of having so many female relatives to visit, let alone live with you, is making you squirm, spare a thought for your darling wife when besieged by your mother and aunts.

Of course, you must pretend to be delighted when your wife invites the female members of her family to tea. You can always escape for an hour or two by inventing a calving cow that needs your assistance. Think of the calving unit as your "haven" where you can sit on a bale and ponder the meaning of life by chewing the cud in unison with the cows.

Chew the cud.

When you devote deep thinking and contemplation to an important subject.

SHALL I COMPARE THEE TO A CIVIL SERVANT?

Unfortunately, it seems farmers were way down the list in terms of what made a "good catch". On 23 November 1949, the *Evening Herald* published an article which argued, quite convincingly, that the ideal husband was a civil servant. That was 70 years ago, but many of the points are still relevant today. The good news is you can learn from them in your bid to become an Ideal Farm Husband.

"It is the very essence of his code to keep his mouth shut and never question the policy of his superiors. Women like those who don't answer back."
Hmm, I'm not so sure it was good advice then or now, but it won't do you any harm to think of your wife as your better half and never answer back. (Unless, perhaps, you have a closed door between you.) The best bet is to say your piece to the cows to get it out of your system.

"He sits down all day and therefore he needs exercise at weekends so he can keep the grass in order. This probably explains why his lawn is like a billiard table."
The civil servant probably had a small garden to look after. Are you really expected to cut the grass in your large garden as well

as ensuring your acres of grass are in tip-top condition for the cows, sheep or goats?

Yes, of course you are; that's what makes you an Ideal Farm Husband. However, you can make it easier for yourself by fencing off part of the garden for the pet lambs. Your spouse will think you have the children's interests at heart as well as providing meat for Sunday dinners. Establish a wild flower meadow to encourage bees and butterflies to flourish so your wife's friends can be impressed by your environmentally friendly garden.

"His salary is always known to his wife and obviously he cannot have a secret reserve."
Believe it or not, farmers were reputed to be tight with money, keeping control of the cheque book and doling out a minimum of "housekeeping money" to wives. Joint bank accounts were rare and many farm women didn't have their names on the cheque book. Men were even known to dip into their wives' pin money from egg sales to pop to the pub – that never went down well. Considering that farm incomes are diminishing further now, I'd say farmers with secret reserves are few and far between.

Ideal farm husbands give their wives access to the bank account, hoping she can create some magic with the overdraft and get it to change colour from red to black.

"His hours are fixed and he can never ring up to say he has been kept late when he really wants a game of cards or a few drinks."
A farmer's hours are never fixed so there's little you can do in this instance. Years ago, farmers incorporated their socialising into a day's work by going to the pub after the mart. It was considered an important part of the day's work as he had to get the buyer a drink and cogitate over the day's sales to see who got a good deal. They had perfect farm wives at home milking cows, feeding pigs, tending to poultry and cooking meals for their children.

Of course, today, it's a very different story regarding drinking alcohol and driving so a farm husband catches up on the news when he gets his dinner in the mart cafe. An ideal farm husband always lets his wife know if he has eaten dinner elsewhere because if she has sweated over cooking a meal, he's going to be in the bad books (unless, of course, he can manage a second dinner).

"He can always be reached by phone at the office and encouraged to bring home messages."
Before the advent of mobile phones, it wasn't easy to contact farmers. They could hide away in distant fields for hours if they wanted to do so. A whistle was used to summon them for dinner or for emergencies. Nowadays, an ideal farm husband has no excuse and must always respond to text messages.

From the 1940s to the 1970s, many farmers did the grocery shopping as lots of women didn't drive. My grandfather drove to Carlow every Thursday no matter what was happening on the farm. He left the shopping list with the shopkeeper and then visited his brother in his radio shop for a couple of hours. When he returned, the shopping was waiting for him packaged up in a couple of boxes. Shopping was a much more civilised affair back then! Some wives travelled to town with their husbands and did the shopping while he was in the pub.

An ideal farm husband always checks if anything is needed from the shops, and if in any doubt, buys chocolate anyway.

"He can take some of his leave on 'odd days' or even half days."
Sometimes you just have to seize the moment and take an unexpected day off away from the farm. Leave those non-urgent, long-finger jobs that will always be there and head to the beach, especially on occasions like Ireland's "one-day heat wave" on 19 July 2016. It will do you all a power of good and you will be held up as an ideal farm husband by wives who aren't as fortunate.

Remember that farmers are self-employed so can take time off at any time – as long as the livestock and crops are of like mind of course.

"She can get him to take a day off and accompany her on a shopping expedition and carry all the parcels."

Hmmm, a tricky one. You can probably understand why a bag carrier would be handy, but realistically no woman really wants her husband hanging around yawning and looking bored, let alone knowing what she is spending. You know waiting around clothes shops gives you backache and you never know where to look.

The best solution is to ask if she would like company and try not to look too relieved when she says no. In case she might say yes, suggest that you want to call into the mart for half an hour on the way and that should get you off the hook.

"He can act as babysitter while she ventures forth on a shopping orgy."

You see, this one is much better. She heads off shopping and you get to stay at home. There are occasions, other than shopping orgies, when you're on parenting duty. Plan your childcare days so that you can have fun with the kids as well as get some gardening or paperwork done while they are napping or "helping" you. Be thankful that not being tied to an office means you have these opportunities to spend time with them and your kids get frequent go-to-work-with-dad days. Just one of the huge benefits of a farming life.

As you can see, some of the qualities that were once admired in civil servants are possible for farmers to emulate. It's just a case of honing those skills!

QUIZ

Test yourself against the ideal husbands of yesteryear

The subject of what makes an ideal husband surfaced again in 1968[4] and, as you'll see, farmers were gaining an edge. See if the selections you make in this multiple choice quiz result in you being able to claim that you would have been viewed as an ideal farm husband in 1968.

An Ideal Husband

1. "He rarely catches cold, and if he should, it is sent about its business, never once encouraged to linger with punch and sympathy for two snivelling weeks."
   (a) You have a wonderful immunity from being exposed to all weathers. ❏
   (b) Someone has to nag you to go to the doctor for check-ups or when you are really sick. ❏
   (c) You admit to getting "man flu" occasionally and taking to the bed for at least a week. ❏

2. "His suits repose on coat hangers in the wardrobe, not in a state of collapse on chair backs, or enduring slow strangulation on a doornail."

    (a) Your suit is in the wardrobe and your farming clothes hang on a doornail. ❑

    (b) Your damp farm coat dries out overnight while hanging on a chair close to the wood burning stove, ensuring the kitchen has a lovely aroma each morning. ❑

    (c) Your dirty clothes are strewn on the floor from the scullery to the bathroom with the debris of dubious materials trailing in their wake. ❑

3. "His shirts are always immaculate."

    (a) Your farm shirts are patterned with vibrant checks so stains aren't that obvious. ❑

    (b) Your collars are ripped, your shirts are stained with dubious substances, and you're missing at least one button from each shirt, exposing a toned six-pack (or not). ❑

    (c) You choose a shirt for the day by picking one up from the floor and sniffing it before putting it on! ❑

4. "His food fads are largely non-existent; he never pampers a neurotic digestion, a device indulged in by men of lesser stature."

    (a) You eat everything put in front of you, always thank the cook and can cook a quick fry up if required. ❑

    (b) You fancy yourself as a Heston Blumenthal and are convinced you would have a good chance of winning MasterChef if only you could get away from the farm. You're never shy about giving culinary advice to anyone who will listen. ❑

    (c) You eat only food that is exactly the same as your mother cooked; in fact, you still go to your mother's house for dinner a few days a week. ❑

5. "He treats newspapers with respect."
    (a) It takes you a week to read the farming newspaper from cover to cover. ❑
    (b) Your farming papers are neatly folded and filed according to date within a magazine rack. ❑
    (c) You fall asleep while reading the paper and it falls, scattering, all over the floor. Your farming papers from the last month litter the end of the table, the floor and sofa. It is only when they have been put in the recycling bin that you recall you meant to tear out an article for future reference. ❑

6. "He avoids such home wrecking comments as 'You never wear that nice little dress you had when we were first married.'"
    (a) You comment only on the clothes she wears now and always with a compliment. ❑
    (b) You keep a tally of all clothes and shoes to ensure that all are worn. Why would she need a new dress for a wedding when that one from three years ago would do perfectly? ❑
    (c) You haven't got a clue what's in her wardrobe and never notice what she wears. ❑

7. "He is always on time for meals but is sufficiently realistic not to expect to be actually adequately fed when a do-it-yourself job, like painting the kitchen is in full bloom."
    (a) You're never on time but if dinner is late, you are happy to grab an apple and go away until it's ready, or sit with the farm paper being careful to stay out of her way. ❑
    (b) You are happy to cook dinner and steam up the kitchen with the deep-fat fryer. ❑
    (c) You come into the kitchen, ask "Is it not ready yet?", moan and get in the way. ❑

The matter of the ideal husband surfaced again in 1989:[5]

8. "One who dies young. It is a whole lot easier to live with a vibrant memory than spreading flesh."

    (a) You deliberately don't have a quad so you stay trim by walking up to 15,000 steps a day around the farm. ❏

    (b) You are a sports fanatic and insist on eating protein with every meal. You farm all day and go training any evening you're not working on the farm. ❏

    (c) You plan on having two full dinners each day – one with your mother and the other with your wife – but are confident you'll stay slim. ❏

9. "He could be a mountainy man with loads of land and no mother-in-law."*

    (a) You own 300 acres with beautiful views of five counties on a fine day. ❏

    (b) Your farm is situated five miles down a grassy boreen so is perfect for those who love solitude. ❏

    (c) You're not moving away from your mother – no one can cook a bacon and cabbage dinner like she does. ❏

    * Note: I do not advocate getting rid of mothers in order to reach perfection.

How did you do?

Mostly A's – Your mother trained you well and you show excellent potential for becoming an Ideal Farm Husband. Bring her out for Sunday lunch as a thank you.

Mostly B's – You're going to need a lot of work. Don't presume this will be easy; there will be cold turkey and tears but we'll get you there.

Mostly C's – My goodness, I'm so glad you got this book; it's the only way you'll reach salvation.

PART TWO

HISTORICAL

WHY SOME FARMERS WEREN'T IDEAL FARM HUSBANDS

To really learn from the past, we're going to explore how some farmers failed miserably in terms of being seen as a good catch let alone becoming an ideal husband. Some must have succeeded and gone on to have long and happy marriages with children to carry on the farm, but the path to true love and perfection didn't always run smooth.

No respect for water

Yes, one problem was as simple as water. The element that is essential for survival, and mighty handy for washing and cooking. The stuff that flows out of the sky regularly here in Ireland. The clear liquid many people see as being free to produce.

I don't mean there wasn't any water, or that farmers wasted it by leaving the taps running when they were brushing their teeth or failed to mend leaks in pipes. The problem was, on many farms there *were* no taps or pipes.

Most townhouses (and a minority of farmhouses) had running water piped to the kitchen and bathroom taps by 1946. Town women could turn a tap and hot or cold water flowed out.

It was a very different story in most Irish farmhouses.[6] Women and children had to walk to a well or pump to collect drinking water in buckets and carry them back to the house. Water for washing was collected from rivers or barrels of rainwater in the yard. This became of public concern when government ministers realised women of marriageable age were being swayed by basic amenities such as piped water and were heading to the towns and cities.

In a Dáil debate in 1945, the minister for agriculture, Dr James Ryan, argued:

> We should aim at having the country house just as well equipped as the city house, so that the farmer will have proper lighting, heating, hot and cold water, proper sanitation and so on, so that if a girl has to make a choice between marrying a farmer and settling down in the country, or settling down in the city, she shall at least have the same amenities in the country as in the town or city.[7]

The lengthy process of collecting water, heating it and then doing the washing-up was described in great detail by the Irish Countrywomen's Association (ICA):

> A farm woman had to fill her kettle with water, which has to be brought in from outside – two stages in the process. Her kettle is likely to be a heavy iron kettle which she must proceed to lift onto the open fire – a third stage. When the water is hot, she lifts the kettle off the fire and pours it into the basin – a fourth stage. She begins to wash her dishes. Soon the water is greasy. She must throw it out and fill up her basin out of the kettle again – a fifth stage. She finishes washing her dishes and dries them. Now her basin is dirty and greasy. She must lift up her kettle again, pour in more hot water if there is any left, rinse her basin and put it away – a sixth stage. She must now refill her kettle

with cold water. Otherwise, if she leaves it near the fire the bottom will be burned out of it – a seventh stage. Likely by this time her pail of cold water is empty and she must go outside the house to fill it up again – the eighth stage. That is to say, apart from the actual washing and drying of the dishes, there have been eight operations to carry out. For the townswoman, there is just one operation in the same process: she stands at her sink and turns on her hot and cold tap as required.[8]

I bet you are tired after reading that as well as realising that heading to a city was a no-brainer for many women. The poor farm woman didn't even get to have a cup of tea after her eight stages of filling that kettle and pouring out the hot water! Put in their shoes, would you choose a married life with hot running water from a tap or the above? He'd want to be a pretty special farmer, wouldn't he? And yes, some of them must have been, but it was a bit daft to rely on charm alone when just getting piped water could have made a man so much more desirable.

By the 1960s, the ICA decided this had gone on long enough. Piped water in farmhouses was as rare as hen's teeth. They advised women not to get married until their potential new home had electricity and piped water. They argued women were being asked to "love, honour and carry water" at a time when the technology was available to get rid of that drudgery.

Yes, you read that right. The technology was available. A grant scheme was even introduced in 1950 to help farmers install a piped water supply and 13,000 farmers had benefited from it by 1959. There were 362,000 farm holdings in Ireland in

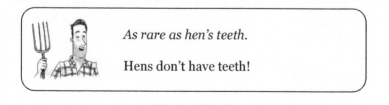

As rare as hen's teeth.

Hens don't have teeth!

19

1960, so what about the rest of them? The NFA (now known as the Irish Farmers' Association) believed rates would increase if piped water added to the value of farms. They even picketed an ICA meeting in Waterford. As a powerful lobbying group, the NFA managed to delay water schemes around the country.[9]

Many newspaper editors tried to make farmers see sense by emphasising the benefits of running water. Numerous articles highlighted that piped water would increase profits by improving dairy hygiene and increasing milk yield. They stressed farming was a team effort between husband and wife: that if women had various labour-saving devices such as piped water, they could add considerably to the farm income. The *Nenagh Guardian* calculated that if her source of water was 100 yards from the house, the farm woman spent 76 cumulative days just walking to and from that well – time that could be spent much more productively![10]

And so marrying a farmer who had these modern conveniences or moving to a town where they were readily available became a preferred choice for many women. And who could blame them?

Tip: Never mock modern conveniences or labour-saving devices or you could find your wife running away from the hills. Remember, a dishwasher is a best friend to many.

Financial concerns

"If you wish to make a million in farming, you need to start with two million."

Farming was tough in many countries during the Great Depression of the 1930s. In Ireland, the Taoiseach's[11] scheme to "starve Britain" by ceasing exports of cattle resulted in the animals becoming almost worthless, thus seriously affecting farm incomes.

It was the small farmers, those with holdings of between one and five acres, who had the poorest living accommodation. In 1926, almost half of these married farmers lived in one-roomed dwellings compared to just over a quarter of labourers.[12] A programme of publicly funded cottage building was ongoing with 16,526 labourers' homes being built between 1932 and 1940. These cottages were relatively comfortable homes with a sizeable garden for growing fruit and vegetables.

The strong farmer with over 30 acres was struggling too, and some women took it upon themselves to write to the editors of national newspapers to highlight the situation.

Irish Independent 4 February 1935

We hear that child labour in cities is forbidden and should not be tolerated, yet no notice is taken of the farmer's child from eleven years of age in rags and tatters shivering with cold and undoubtedly underfed, picking and sowing potatoes etc. and helping generally on the farm from morning until night on a diet of porridge and milk for breakfast and potatoes and milk for dinner.

The farmer rears a batch of calves and may lose most if not all in a few days from black leg etc. The very animal he has for sale becomes unsaleable in a few hours (if there is such a thing as a cattle sale nowadays). He may seek the vet's aid (it is costly) but very seldom will circumstances permit to have a doctor for himself, his wife or children, until it is too late.

Reading about such circumstances in national newspapers or seeing it first-hand wasn't really going to compel young women to marry farmers unless they were madly in love or believed the situation would improve in time.

Tip: Never complain that "there's no money in farming": she might believe it and run a mile.

A country of old men

Most farmers could afford to get married only when they were, let's say, past their prime. Set in their ways, not necessarily with a full set of teeth and with little dress sense, they weren't going to set young hearts alight. And it was young women who could bear them children that they wanted to marry. Unfortunately for them, many of those young women had other ideas and left the countryside in search of jobs, independence and younger husbands as soon as they could. The shortage of women willing to marry farmers in some parts of the country led to much concern about the number of bachelors and the lack of children to take over family farms.

But why did men leave it so late before thinking of marriage? Before the Great Famine of the 1840s, large families were able to survive on small farms due to their dependence on the potato for food. Farms were divided and subdivided among sons so families in the West were surviving on tiny plots of a quarter of an acre. When families starved because their crops of potatoes failed, many believed it was the Irish method of inheritance that was partly to blame for such a tragedy. After that, most farm households decided that the farm could support just one family, and one child (usually a son) inherited.

The successor had to wait until his father died or retired before he could marry and have a family of his own. This went on for a couple of generations. Often men were well into middle age before they could consider marriage, sometimes three or four decades older than the women they courted. Talk about being the cat that got the cream! They may not have been as physically appealing as a strapping muscular 28-year-old, but given that marriage brought status and a home to call their own some women were happy with the arrangement.

The cat that got the cream.

When someone is really pleased at having accomplished something. Self-satisfied.

Too much like hard work

The vast majority of married women in Ireland could not work outside the home until the marriage bar was lifted in 1973. The life of a "town housewife" was very different from that of a farmer's wife in the 1950s and 1960s. The townswoman was encouraged to keep her home spotless and decorated following the latest trends, to ensure her children were well-behaved, her cooking commendable and her husband's comforts prioritised. She was under pressure from magazines and marriage manuals to have her hair coiffured, a hot dinner waiting and children ready for bed when he came home from work. She was considered lazy, selfish and disorganised if she expected her husband to help with the washing-up after a hard day in the office. Maura Laverty, agony aunt at *Woman's Way*, thought it "most unfair to expect the breadwinner to wash dishes".[13]

As the town wife was soothing her husband's brow when he got home from work, the farm wife was just getting second wind. She was heading out to the yard to hand-milk cows, feed calves and pigs, shut in poultry and carry water; then she would return to the house to prepare tea, put children to bed, wash up and eventually sit down at the fire to darn socks or knit a jumper for one of her many children.

Indeed, if a man thought he could afford to be choosy, he often looked for evidence of a hard worker. Mr J McA of Dublin married a girl he "saw for the first time while she was sewing buttons on an old shirt".[14] A Scottish farmer recalled the first time he saw his wife: she was sitting with a group of other girls and as he knew one of them to be a secretary he assumed they all were until he noticed one had welly marks[15] on her legs and decided "that will do me".[16]

Although some farmers' daughters stated in their personal advertisements that they wanted to meet a farmer's son, many others were adamant they weren't interested in a farmer. Farmers weren't exactly renowned for having a good income either, so some women set their cap at men in other professions. According to a matchmaker in 1955, many rural women scorned small farmers, favouring instead police, national school teachers, or indeed any well-paid individuals.[17] Money talked. If a woman could afford to be fussy, she was!

> ### *Irish Independent* 11 May 1940
> Respectable farmer's daughter, 34 years, wishes to correspond with respectable gentleman. Meath or Westmeath preferred. Dowry £500. Strict privacy.

Farmers' daughters knew they would end up doing the bulk of the yard work. Some commentators didn't realise that this was an issue for women and thought the problem of low marriage rates among farmers was related to men not seeing the advantages of having a wife and did their utmost to point out the benefits.

> No need for an alarm clock in the morning. Someone to milk the cows, fodder the cattle, dig the spuds, make the hay, clean out the pigs. Someone to cook, sew and sow, to cuddle and fondle and have kids by, to clean up the place, talk to the crusty neighbours, attend the local ICA meeting.[18]

You'd wonder what on earth he did apart from sit by the fire!

Tip: Thinking of cutting out that paragraph about the 1960s' wife and showing it to your partner? Don't.

The in-laws

It was expected that young couples would share the farmhouse with the in-laws. In 1969, a young housewife claimed that the bachelor farmers were not to blame for the high rate of late marriages. She put some of the blame on the "would-be farmers' brides" who were reluctant to move in with their in-laws. She claimed she had the best father-in-law and mother-in-law in the world.[19] It has to be said, though, this was a minority view. "Girls don't want to marry into such homes even if wanted there. The eldest son is often last to be married as he must wait until the house is cleared."[20]

> **Western People 13 November 1991**
> An old father or mother in the house was not an asset, particularly a mother; an old woman could be an awkward customer for a daughter-in-law to come in to live with; in most cases an old man was easier to put up with.

In the 1940s, Taoiseach Éamon de Valera, concerned at the dwindling number of rural marriages, had tried to introduce a "dower-house scheme" whereby a second farm property would be publicly funded, but it never came to pass. It wasn't until much later in the century that the two generations lived separately in most situations. The reputation of the mother-in-law was fearsome and, in some families, endures.

Don't worry, I'm not going to suggest you get rid of your dear mum, but you might need to read the section on ensuring your mother and your wife get on well!

Penny pinching

Even with its tongue-in-cheek humour there seems to be more than a nugget of truth in the following article; some men just didn't want to spend money on a woman.

> **Longford Leader 26 May 1978**
> Arguably the greatest waste of male power is manifested through the heads of bachelor farmers who doggedly refuse to tie the knot. Could it be that

they value the purchase of a beautiful Friesian heifer more than they would the amount of money they'd have to spend to turn their present living quarters into something a self-respecting female wouldn't spring away from? Is it that they just don't like the patter of female feet around the dunghill, ah, no, not queer, just independent and fond of their dirt.

This writer definitely isn't portraying these men in the best light. I'm guessing these bachelor farmers didn't have running water yet either, let alone a bath tub!

Apart from being reluctant to spend money on wives or the house, men often controlled the farm income from cattle, milk and crops. Women may have received "housekeeping" money to buy essentials but frequently didn't have a say over the finances. Women made butter and sold eggs not just to have some "pin money" but to contribute much needed money to the farm income. For women who wanted some financial independence, this type of farmer certainly wasn't ideal.

Tip: Remember those vows you make on marriage: "What's mine is yours"!

Prerequisites for marriage

In the 1950s marriage was quite an achievement for farmers, with over 33% of farming males aged 35–44 being single.[21] It was something to strive for since married men commanded more respect in small communities. Before he could get married, a man had to prove he could support a family.

How did a farmer persuade the lady he wanted to marry that he was an eligible bachelor, a good catch, worthy of her and the making of an ideal farm husband? It wasn't a case of falling in love and living happily ever after on the land. In fact, there was often no mention of love or attraction or chemistry. So exactly what did a single farmer need to have in place in order to attract a wife?

Death

Not his own, obviously. In many parts of the country a single farmer had to wait until his father was dead or retired before he could consider marriage, as the farm couldn't afford to support two families. This meant that many farmers were in their 50s or 60s before they got married.

For some, leaving it so late meant it didn't happen. The eligible women had either left the parish or were too old to have children. Bachelor farmers sometimes led lonely lives then, particularly if they lived a distance from neighbours and had only a bicycle, an ass and cart or a small tractor for transport.[22]

Money

Once he had inherited the farm, he had to show the parents of a prospective wife that he had the means to support a family and convince them to part with a significant sum of money or valuable possessions in the form of a dowry along with their daughter.

What did he need the dowry for? Was it to build a new house, a modern milking parlour, more cowsheds, or to buy new-fangled machinery? No, the dowry didn't necessarily improve the finances of the couple but was often used to fund a dowry for one of his sisters. According to an article in *The Englishwoman*:

> As many as a dozen nuptial knots have been known to be tied by means of one and the same £100. Tim O'Donoghue gets a fortune of £100, clear of marriage dues and wedding expenses, with his wife. The money is then handed over by his parents to Ned McCabe, who marries their daughter, Mary Kate. Ned McCabe

passes on the £100 to his own sister, Julia, who thereby secures a mate in Terence McGrath; and Terence's sister, Agnes, by its agency, becomes Mrs Maurice Doogan. So this identical £100 passes on, marrying all the eligible girls in the townsland, leaving joy, happiness and contentment in its wake, just as if it were a beneficent fairy with a wand of enchantment.[23]

However, this "wand of enchantment" meant men weren't prepared or able to marry without a dowry. Marriage wasn't for love; it was a business transaction designed to strengthen family alliances and sometimes to increase farm size. It was expected that the couple would live in harmony and support each other. When placing a personal advertisement in the newspapers, farmers reduced the risk of wasting time in having to respond to "unsuitable women" by explicitly stating that finances in the shape of a dowry or a farm were required. Anything less was not going to pass muster.

Irish Examiner 7 January 1961

Farmer with good, well-stocked farm in nice locality, wishes to hear from girl over 30, who is anxious to settle down in the near future. Dowry essential. All answers treated with confidence and returned.

It seems it was a truth universally acknowledged that a single woman in possession of a good farm must be in want of a husband. #misquote

Second or third sons, not inheriting at home but wanting to farm, sometimes looked for a wife with her own farm. To be accepted by her family, he needed to bring money with him.

***Irish Examiner* 28 July 1962**

Farmer's son with a large dowry, wishes to meet farmer's daughter with farm of her own, with nice appearance; view to matrimony, strictly private.

A man marrying into a good farm was often described as "being on the pig's back"!

As time moved on, dowries disappeared. Once the marriage bar was lifted in 1973, allowing women with professions to continue working after marriage, nurses and teachers became the preferred choice for many[24] – jobs that would provide a steady and good income with a pension.

Romance seems to have been scarce back then, with marriage being a financial transaction. Nowadays, farmers are sometimes accused of not being romantic (yes, really!) but I wonder if that's a throwback to the days when they were discouraged from being romantic and were expected to be practical in their marriage choice.

On the pig's back.

To be prosperous, especially when it is not through your own efforts, e.g. inheriting or marrying into a farm. It is a literal translation of the Irish phrase *ar mhuin na muice*, a colloquialism to mean well off or happy.

No dependants

If a single man had his mother or siblings living with him, their presence often delayed a marriage. Many couples were engaged for years waiting for siblings to move away or get married, hence the eldest (the son who usually inherited the farm) was often the last to be married.[25] If he didn't have any dependants, he advertised the fact.

Irish Press 27 May 1954
Farmer, Catholic, 38, good farm, considered good looking, no incumbrance, wishes introduction with good-looking lady having capital or farm. Farmer's daughter preferred.

Irish Examiner 12 April 1952
Farmer, 36 years, TT, quiet disposition, no incumbrances, wishes to meet farmer's daughter, view to marriage, strict confidence.

Having no siblings or a prospective mother-in-law was clearly an advantage worth using as a hook.

Modern conveniences

We know the lack of water facilities was a problem, but what about old ranges, thatched roofs and stone floors? With the advent of women's magazines, women could see the advantages of refrigerators, vacuum cleaners and electric cookers, not to mention a sink with taps. Molly Bawn seems to have all bases covered:

Irish Farmers Journal 19 March 1966
Molly Bawn is a Longford farmer's daughter. Early 30s, non-drinker and non-smoker, would like to get in touch with a farmer 36–40 with his own farm and modern home, from midland counties with view to marriage. Snaps please.

Although many women couldn't afford the modern conveniences advertised in women's magazines, they still wanted them and the advertisers worked hard to emphasise the advantages. They even compared the home lives of men – the man with the electric cooker in his kitchen could relax reading the newspaper whereas the man with the old range had to spend time each year painting the kitchen.[26] Women were shown how a freezer would give them more free time as they wouldn't have to shop as frequently and could buy and freeze in bulk. Farm women could certainly see the advantages in a freezer for preserving the meat from their own livestock as well as the surplus fruit and vegetables from their gardens.[27]

A draughty old farmhouse without electricity, let alone little hope of an electric cooker, a freezer or a man who would paint the kitchen, was becoming a barrier for some women.

Teetotaller

Why was being a non-drinker important? Well, given the Irish propensity for alcohol, with men spending considerable sums at the pub, being a teetotaller could give a man an advantage in the marriage stakes. Although some brides' families weren't fussy once the hurdle of having a farm and means to marry were passed, some women were becoming more demanding as time went on. There was an increase in the number of men advertising their teetotal (TT) status in the 1960s.

> **Irish Press 9 August 1962**
> Respectable farmer's son, cattle dealer, with priest in family and highest PP references, strict TT, would like to meet farmer's daughter with farm of her own, or girl with business shop in the country, all letters answered, strict confidence given.

This farmer's son is setting his cap high looking for a woman with considerable assets so he's emphasising all of the qualities he believes would help his case. Who could resist?

References

As in the personal advertisement above, a reference from a parish priest (PP) was seen as advantageous too. (Even better was having a priest or a nun in the family.) Even a bank manager's reference was cited and demanded!

Irish Examiner 6 January 1912

The guardian of a respectable well educated farmer's daughter, about 30 years, with a fortune of £1,000 and a small farm, would like to hear from a respectable business man with an income, not less than 30 years, or a respectable, independent farmer with a good farm, view matrimony. PP and bank references will be required.

This must have turned the first contact into an interview. Imagine asking your bank manager to write a reference proving you're a safe bet and not too heavily overdrawn. I'm not sure which is harder to picture: the request, or a farmer without an overdraft. You certainly wouldn't want to be bashful!

The right religion

Mixed religion marriages were at best frowned upon and at worst forbidden. Religion was as much a divider as class. Just as a "strong farmer" wouldn't permit a daughter to marry a landless labourer, marrying someone of another religion wasn't approved either, so the person's religion was cited in many personal advertisements.

Irish Examiner 4 December 1948

Respectable farmer's son, Protestant, with sixty acres land, five miles from Cork, wishes to hear from Protestant girl with view to marriage.

Irish Examiner 21 September 1954

Catholic young man, with £1,400 capital wishes to meet girl under 30 years of age with business or farm with view to matrimony.

Sons and daughters were often threatened with being disinherited if they dared marry someone of another religion. Stating the "required" religion in an advertisement avoided time-wasting.

Good health

There was little point in marrying a "lady who lunches" type back then. There was too much work to be done on the farm. A prospective groom's family wouldn't countenance anything less than a wife who was hale and hearty. She had to come from "good stock", have no symptoms of disease (TB or insanity were seen as the greatest impediments) and be young enough to bear children. Scandals within the family were a no-no too.[28]

Becoming a husband wasn't just a case of finding the love of your life at a local dance. A host of hurdles had to be overcome first. No wonder so many stayed single. Luckily, help was at hand, as you'll discover in the next section.

PART THREE

FINDING A WIFE

TRADITIONAL WAYS
TO FIND A WIFE

Personal ads

As you've probably guessed with all the examples of personal advertisements, this was a much-used method of finding a suitable partner. Those placing the ads were quite emphatic in their likes and dislikes as well as blowing their own trumpet.

> **Irish Press 15 March 1963**
> Wealthy respectable Roscommon farmer, late forties, desires acquaintance with sincere girl, 30–35, interested in farming, confidential.

Once the 1960s arrived, there were signs of more independence from women with some hints at equality. They weren't describing their sum of money as a dowry but as their own possession, not something to be handed over. A farmer eagerly reading through some of these advertisements would be disappointed to discover he was ineligible.

> **Irish Press 15 March 1963**
> Lady, educated convent boarding school, slim, attractive, capital £1,000, wishes to hear from business or professional gentleman in his fifties, genuinely interested in early marriage.

Women often asked for men in specific professions, particularly if they were in a position to choose because they had secured a profession like nursing or teaching or they were in possession of a good dowry. Even farmers' daughters weren't always interested in marrying farmers.

Irish Examiner 30 May 1953
Farmer's Daughter (RC) good appearance and address with £1,200 dowry, wishes to meet a respectable RC shopkeeper or government official with a view to matrimony.

There's no mention of GSOH; interests in sports such as GAA, football or swimming; hobbies such as hill walking, dancing or music; cinema; travelling; cooking or eating out. Personal advertisements were very factual and focused. I don't think being as forthright in an advertisement today would work!

Matchmaking

While parents were instrumental in deciding whether or not a marriage went ahead in the past, they often secured help from a matchmaker. So how did it work?

Charlie Carberry, a well-known matchmaker in the early to mid twentieth century, made it his business to attend the fairs between Christmas and Shrove Tuesday.[29] This was the busiest time of the year as marriages were not permitted between Ash Wednesday and Easter. Engagements were short, so if a man wanted to get married before Easter, "when a young man might be considering the advisability of having a wife for splitting potatoes or feeding the pet lambs later on",[30] he had to be on the lookout just after Christmas.

Charlie had two reasons to be at the fairs: he knew prospective grooms or their fathers would make contact with him there, buying him a drink to signal their interest, but he was also noting the prices being achieved in the sales of cattle so he knew how much to bargain when it came to the negotiations.

Language was subtle. A man didn't state he wanted to marry a particular girl. A prospective groom or his father would indicate their interest by saying something like "so and so's daughter is a powerful hand at a soda cake". If the matchmaker considered her suitable, he went to her father's house with a bottle of whiskey. If her father was interested, negotiations began.[31]

If a groom's father hadn't identified a potential bride, he asked a matchmaker to source one.

> Like a shopman who can immediately locate many of his wares in his shop, the matchmaker from the profundity of his wide knowledge suggests four or five suitable names. The possibilities of each are discussed; every aspect is considered – family, hereditary traits, appearance, reputation, means, incumbrances and what not? Finally one name is singled out and operations are to be begun on this one.[32]

Love was rarely mentioned. Lisdoonvarna matchmaker Willie Daly recalled a mother and son visiting him for matchmaking services and when he asked the son what kind of a wife he wanted, the mother replied with a brusque "What Michael needs now is a woman who can help him up the mountain with the sheep and the cows."[33] There was no room for sentiment!

HV Morton, an English writer travelling around Ireland in the 1920s, recounted the showmanship, pomp and circumstance in the negotiations once both parties showed interest.

> The boy's spokesman, backed by the others began praising the suitor: how he had a well-stocked farm; was sober as well as rich; had no brothers to divide his inheritance. To this the bride's party answered by praising the girl, as industrious and skilled in the arts

of needlework. In the upshot the hundred pounds was agreed to. Then a new discussion arose as to whether it should be in stock or in cash, and the award was made at sixty pounds in cash, and cattle to the value of forty. Then the stock had to be discussed and specified. Lastly, the father dealt with the question of the ceremonial heifer, which is always given with the bride by any father who wishes to hold up his head in the country. ... And in truth there is no society where marriage is more a matter of arrangement than among the Irish Catholic tillers of the soil – and none where the marriage-tie is more binding.[34]

Once the matter of the dowry was settled, it was time for the "plucking of the gander". Representatives from the girl's family visited the young man's farm to inspect premises and stock in case he had lied about his farm and possessions. The numbers of chains in the cow house were counted in case the farmer had borrowed cattle from a neighbour. This deception would be similar to you bringing a new girlfriend to a rented mansion and pretending it was yours! He was expected to keep his wife in the way in which she was accustomed or even a step up the social ladder. Once the agreements were finalised, the wedding plans started.[35]

It can certainly seem cold and matter-of-fact to us today, yet it was seen as normal by the Irish. Visitors were shocked though; Morton seemed appalled at the business-like arrangement of marrying for land and described it as "deliberate, cold-blooded unsentimentalism".[36]

If families didn't have cash, the dowry could be a donkey, cows, chickens, pigs or furniture. Occasionally the negotiations didn't go so well. Prospective engagements ended, not because of a falling out between the couple, but because a father wouldn't give as much as the groom wanted. Here's an example from the memoir *The Farm by Lough Gur*:[37]

I remember overhearing my father enquiring of old Paddy about a projected match.

"Tel me Paddy, did Johnnie make the match for his daughter?"

"He did not, sir, though 'twas very near done when they bruk it clean off."

"And what broke it?"

"'Twas the ass and car that defeated it. Ould Johnnie wouldn't part with the ass, though the ould woman was content to let it go. So his darter is disapp'inted of a home and young Johnnie is disapp'inted of a wife."

"I'm sorry," said my father, who had a kind heart for all young things.

"There's no need," replied Paddy, "no need at all. There's more than one fish in Lough Gur, and the matchmaker is on the trail of another for the both of them."

Therefore, a person's life partner could be changed depending on how the negotiations went. If you wanted a few extra hens along with your wife and they weren't forthcoming, you might have decided to look elsewhere for a better deal!

As weddings were arranged by elders, it was often the case that the young couple hadn't met before the wedding day and scarcely recognised each other after the festivities were over.

A farmer married a local girl that he hardly knew. After the wedding he approached a group of girls standing outside the church. "Whichever one of you I married, will you come on home. The cattle need milking!"[38]

One can't help but sense the nervousness, desperation and disappointment that this bride experienced on her wedding day:

Mother was resting after attending the wedding of a neighbour's daughter, who did not know which of two brothers she was to marry until she stood before the altar and saw *the wrong one* by her side.[39]

While Morton saw it as cold, calculating and business-like, there were those that saw it as much more sensible than following one's heart and falling in love with an unknown.

Irish Examiner 20th December 1955

He could not understand the mentality of young people today who fix up their future under the light of a full moon and would abuse or turn a deaf ear to anyone who suggested they were incapable of taking such an important decision in so casual a way. These young people were not beyond asking a friend's advice in the purchase of a second-hand car, or taking a hairdresser's suggestion on the shade of lipstick to suit their complexion but when it came to making a lasting decision as to their life partner, well these very people were their own capable advisors.

Matchmakers were confident in their success rates, claiming they had studied both partners from the point of view of suitability to each other in status, financial position and temperament.

One matchmaker, the famous Dan Paddy Andy O'Sullivan, measured his success by the number of children born to a couple, claiming that a big family proved the match to be very fruitful as well as happy. He boasted he had not had a failed marriage in all the matches he organised in 30 years of matchmaking. Given his success, he offered to help a priest with the marriage problems of his Kerry parish, where there had been only two weddings in the previous four years.[40]

Some people viewed it in harsher terms than Morton, describing matchmaking as unethical, as trafficking women, as pushing young women into impossibly sad situations.

Ballina Herald 24 October 1936

There are lots of cases of incurable misery brought
about by an unnatural union. Nobody benefits by this
traffic in womanhood – even materially – in the end.

The young girl, whose father walks her and her
one or two hundred pounds of a fortune, into a place
already swamped with debt, is indeed to be pitied. The
moment her money is gone paying off creditors she
becomes a burden. Her mother-in-law might deny her
a say in the running of the house.

And, indeed, unfortunately some marriages weren't happy. A
widow from County Cavan claimed that the day her husband
died was the happiest in her life.[41]
Traditional matchmaking died out slowly although
arranged marriages still took place as late as the early 1970s.
Willie Daly of Lisdoonvarna has kept it going, although he
admitted in 1994 it was becoming much more difficult as
women were more independent and hence much fussier.[42]

Ballrooms of romance

Ballrooms of romance were an important meeting place for
couples and laid the foundation for many a relationship that
developed into marriage. The dance halls, situated in small
rural towns, were usually galvanised, round-roofed sheds with a
concrete block front. Women sat on one side and men stood on
the other, having to cross the floor to ask a woman to dance,
which must have been intimidating for many. When the night
was over, the lights came back on revealing the tawdry
surroundings, and people cycled back home along the lanes.

There are also stories of single women who cycled there
every week until into their thirties, when they resigned
themselves to spinsterhood, too old to emigrate.

But that was then and this is now. How have things changed?

HOW CAN *YOU* MEET THE LOVE OF YOUR LIFE?

Farm organisations

Farming organisations for young people were created to promote education within agriculture. They weren't necessarily invented to provide farmers with a place to meet suitable partners but turned out to be very successful at it.

Macra na Feirme in Ireland is for those aged 18–35 interested in rural life and it boasts many marriages. The UK has Young Farmers clubs for those aged 14–26 and many married couples first met at Young Farmers events and balls.

The only problem is, if you haven't met your partner by the time you've reached the age for exiting, there doesn't seem to be similar groups for those in older age groups.

Agricultural shows

There are agricultural shows on almost every weekend during the summer months and well into September so you have plenty of opportunities. You could leave things to chance and see if you might just bump into the love of your life across a crowded field or you could prepare as much as you possibly can. Remember the expression "fail to prepare, prepare to fail", so give it some consideration beforehand.

What kind of woman would you like to meet? If you're looking for someone interested in cooking, for example, you need to go to the tents with food demonstrations and celebrity chefs. She will be in there with hundreds of other women so you will need to look hard for a potential mate. However, if she sees you in that tent, she's going to presume you're interested in cooking too so don't think you'll get away with just setting the table in the future.

If she's competing in the ploughing or animal classes, be prepared to get in the queue as she'll be the perfect catch for any farmer. To impress her, you'll probably have to be competing as well and that takes years of preparation. Don't be afraid to try though as it could be a marriage made in heaven. What could be more couply than getting up early to get your pedigree cattle ready for a show together? Another advantage is the perfect gift will always be a new pedigree calf or lamb so there will be no need for panicking at the jewellery shop window.

Her footwear is a good marker as to her suitability as a farm wife. Unless it is very hot and dry, she is likely to be wearing boots of some description:

- Plain blue or green, or even a Dunbar welly in pink, suggests she purchased them at the creamery so you'll know she is accustomed to working on a farm.

- Brand new and multi-coloured or floral, indicates she probably bought them for the Electric Picnic or borrowed them from a friend; they've only been used to splash in puddles until now but she is prepared for some mud.

- Hunters or a similar brand might hint that you need to have room and stabling for a horse.

The mart

To be honest, you're unlikely to meet a female love of your life at an Irish mart, although it's not entirely unknown. Irish marts still tend to be male-dominated. You'd hope it wouldn't happen in this age, but some women feel they'd be disadvantaged whether selling or bidding so tend to get a man in their family to do that on their behalf.

I'm informed that marts in the UK are more popular with women so there might be more scope there. However, there will be lots of competition! You never know, but don't have the mart as number one in your quest to find a willing partner.

Social media

Social media is all about being sociable. It's where you get the chance to chat online, to show people what your farm is like, share photographs, ask advice, tease others, chat about favourite television programmes, find out what others think about a TV documentary or a recent news event and possibly meet the love of your life.

Ensure your Twitter avatar contains a nice, friendly and up-to-date photograph. You can make it a selfie with one of your animals for a bit of fun. Create an interesting bio so it piques people's interest and encourages them to start a conversation with you. "Farmer, single, milks cows, Kilkenny, views are my own" is unlikely to gain much interest, plus who else's views are they likely to be? "Dairy farmer with a few sheep, love to travel when the cows let me, always half right" is much more likely to be a conversation starter. It invites questions such as where might you travel next, what countries have you visited, what breed are your sheep and when are you half wrong?

It is important that you behave as normal, be yourself, and don't pretend to be someone you're not. There's nothing as off-putting as meeting someone in real life and finding they don't resemble their online persona in looks or deeds.

You can establish what a potential girlfriend is like from her tweets too. If she tweets that she would like to marry a farmer because she thinks it's a life of gathering wild flowers, log fires and chasing butterflies on sunny summer days, you're probably better off giving her a miss unless you're confident you can keep her in the style in which she wants to become accustomed! Don't be afraid to initiate a conversation in response to the tweet of anyone you'd like to get to know better – female or male.

Can you use Twitter to find a soulmate? Well, I have seen a farmer searching for a wife with the tweet "Wife needed to subsidise dairy farmer. Long hours, no pay, secretarial skills a necessity". His tweet got lots of attention but I haven't heard yet if it was successful in securing a wife!

Facebook is still the most commonly used social media platform, a place for people to stay in contact with friends and see what they are up to wherever they are in the world. There are numerous Facebook groups set up for farmers, mainly to discuss farming issues and support each other. Again, it's about being normal rather than stalking someone!

If you're looking for an Irish girl, you can ask if your photo and description can be uploaded onto the "Farmers Daughter blog" Facebook page and see if you can get any interest from prospective girlfriends! Be prepared though: it seems that you need at least 300 acres, plenty of road frontage and a brand new tractor to be in the running!

You just never know what might happen on social media regarding romance. I know of two couples happily married with babies after meeting this way.

Online dating agencies

Online dating agencies provide an online space for you to meet others and if you decide you like each other, you can arrange to meet in person. To be as successful as possible, do submit a recent and good photograph of yourself (not one that looks like a mugshot taken at a police station) and make your profile stand out. Don't tell lies, don't pretend you are 38 when you're 46 or that you are 6 foot 3 if you're only 5 foot 9 – what are you going to do the first time you meet her – wear platforms?

Be specific about your likes too. Saying you like sport could mean anything. You might like watching it on television and playing football once a week with some mates, or it could be whole weekends of fitness training. Some women will put up with the former or be very attracted to the latter (there will be those who would run a mile too). There's no point in meeting up with someone who trains for marathons and expects you to be fit if your only running is when cattle escape from their field.

Choose the right dating site for you. As a farmer, use sites where women are looking for farmers and country types. Examples include *Muddy Matches* in Ireland and the UK and *Farmers Only* in the US.

Knock Marriage Bureau

Knock Marriage Bureau was founded in 1968 and is still going strong. They boast 925 marriages from the 18,068 couples that met since it started almost 50 years ago. It's a mixture of a dating agency and a matchmaking service as they assess the information provided on application forms and suggest introductions. It still has a religious background as you must be Roman Catholic and free to get married within a Roman Catholic Church.

Matchmaking

Is matchmaking something you would consider in your quest to find a suitable and willing partner? You can still go to Lisdoonvarna, Ireland's famous matchmaking festival, in September. People go for the dancing, the drinking and the craic as well as the matchmaking. If the prospect of a noisy drinking scene horrifies you, there are nature walks arranged for single people across the beautiful scenery of the Burren during the Lisdoonvarna festival.

There are a growing number of matchmaking businesses specifically for people who want to meet a special someone. Just as matchmakers in the past looked at personalities and family traits (as well as finances) to create a match, matchmakers today do the same. They interview you in depth; match you to a person with similar likes, dislikes, wants, needs, values and outlook on life. Sometimes we don't know ourselves as well as we think we do and a stranger's input might send us in an unexpected and pleasant direction. Just as matchmakers commanded a fee in the past, today's matchmaking services incur a cost too.

Your own farm

While I wouldn't recommend using this as an excuse not to go looking for your perfect partner, there is a chance she might walk into your yard someday. There are more and more women working as nutritionists, relief milkers and veterinary surgeons and in agri-sales, so you never know. Rather than you riding to her rescue on a white horse, she might drive into your yard in a jeep someday and sweep you off your feet. And on a positive note, if she sees you looking frazzled on a busy day, she knows what's in store for evermore.

I know of three women who worked on farms and ended up marrying the farmer. Yes, he was able to suss out if she was a good worker and she was able to assess his mood as well as everything else, so if you're employing someone, you just never know. I've also heard of those working as milk recorders marrying dairy farmers. Hearing that "their eyes met across the milking pit, lit up by bright fluorescent tubes as they dodged cow poo" doesn't quite have a romantic ring but it worked.

Brian and I met at a rural disco – yes, something like a "ballroom of romance" – way back in 1988. I was going out with someone else at the time but as I liked the look of Brian, I got a mutual friend to introduce us. It took almost a full year for romance to blossom though.

PART FOUR

SEX APPEAL

HOW TO IMPRESS YOUR NEW GIRLFRIEND

You have found the love of your life. You know farming is a great life but you've heard some women have reservations about dating farmers while others have somewhat idealistic notions of the lifestyle. Is it possible to show her the real you, a genuine representation of farming life and still impress her?

How to be sexy

Yeah, okay, you might think you've got this one nailed. Farmers – sexy? Of course! And the good news is: lots of people think so. However, it wasn't always that way. Farmers have been stereotyped in different ways according to their nationality, the media's interests and the value the stereotype imparts to a brand. Sounds contrived, political and somewhat scary? Oh yes. But you can use these labels to your own advantage.

Farmer stereotypes in the past

Irish farmers

Gabriel Byrne brought the notion of a sexy farmer to our screens when he was in the series of *Bracken*.[43] When *Glenroe* started in 1983, things took a dip in terms of the levels of sexiness, with Miley and Dinny Byrne representing farmers on television.

Dinny was a bit of an auld divil; he was always trying to get one over on others. However, he was a decent auld sod representing older farmers. He wore a "sports coat" with braces holding up his trousers and a peaked cap. He never did much work but was a master of leaning on his shepherd's crook and telling everyone else how to do the job properly.

Miley his son, through his kind, well-meaning and rather gullible nature suggested many farmers were just like that. Although more modern in his fashion sense as he wore jeans and a jumper, he wasn't going to set too many hearts aflutter.

A more fearsome stereotype was Bull McCabe in the play *The Field*, a domineering man whose attachment to the land overshadowed everything else until the ultimate price was paid – the loss of life.

Australian farmers

Sheep farmers on huge ranches, using horses, quads and small planes to round up the livestock. The farmer himself is lean and muscular, a talented horseman and an efficient sheep shearer, and while the hat with the bobbing corks to keep flies away is an exaggeration, he will have headgear of some description.

American farmers

A cross between the checked-shirt-and-dungaree-wearing hillbilly country bumpkin and the Texan rancher with his wide-brimmed cowboy hat, checked shirt, leather chaps over denim jeans, big belt buckle, cowboy boots and maybe a handkerchief scarf around his neck. Naturally he is either riding a horse or driving a big pickup truck. *Dallas, John Wayne* westerns and the *Beverly Hillbillies* have a lot to answer for, I think.

British farmers

British farmers were often typecast as the stiff upper lip, gentrified, tweed-wearing, estate-owning English country gent. A rustic squire spending most of his time shooting with his guests rather than milking his cows. Yes, period dramas might influence that one.

Another stereotype is the simple impoverished farmer, quite similar to Irish ones, with his old clothes and peaked cap, who speaks in deference to the aforementioned estate owner. *All Creatures Great and Small* from years ago has a lot to answer for with this vision.

Are your images any different?

Farmer stereotypes in the present

Are you, like the creators of the stereotypes from the past, thinking of the farmer as male, even today? If you ask someone to describe a farmer, they are likely to conjure up the image of a male, over 40 and with calloused hands. But there are also younger farmers and let's not forget the female farmers too.

It's not easy to find a female farmer in the farming papers at times, although new TV programmes focusing on farming are featuring women as well as men. The *Farmers Weekly* runs a "Britain's Sexiest Farmer" competition with two winners – one male, one female. However, we still have some work to do before most people will picture a woman when they hear the word "farmer". The new-age farmer is usually depicted as male, rugged and hard-working, honest and muscular, reverent and caring, trustworthy and tough, able to work the soil and care for his animals. Where do we see those portrayals?

Farming calendars

Farmers are shown to be toned and fit in photo calendar shoots. The Irish Farmer Calendar may not feature them as tanned (yes, the Irish tend to have pale skin on the parts the sun doesn't see) but they are portrayed as strong, game for a laugh, with smiling eyes, and of course, sexy. Indeed, they became so popular they now feature in a book as well.[44]

The 2103 Super Bowl ad for Ram Trucks entitled "So God Made a Farmer"

Within this two-minute commercial, we see young farmers, old farmers, weather-beaten farmers and female farmers. We see their smiling eyes, wrinkles and calloused hands. We view their family mealtimes, their livestock, their fields and their produce. We know from the images and the descriptions that farmers are trustworthy, responsible, strong, patriotic, powerful, honourable, resourceful, faithful, heroic, reverent, moral, creative, civic-minded, and yes, sexy.

As Funda argues in her TEDx talk, this advertisement, with its two minutes of praise for farmers and its 15-second shot of the Ram Truck at the end, endowed that brand with all of those ideals. That was the reason behind the creation of the advertisement of course, but at the same time it ensured that "farming is the new sexy".[45]

Isn't that lucky for you?

Advertisements for supermarkets and fast-food outlets

Just as the "Know Your Food, Know Your Farmer" campaign took off in the US, companies this side of the pond have also been showcasing individual farmers. They want to show consumers who is producing the sumptuous beef (and other foods) they are purchasing.

These male farmers are usually photographed standing on top of a grassy hill on a sunny day with their prize cattle dotted around the field. They are shown to be masterful of their surroundings, caring, strong, determined, trustworthy, reliable, hard-working, rugged, honourable, able to rear good-quality stock from their wholesome grass, salt of the earth types and yes, of course, sexy.

So while stereotypes in the past weren't exactly complimentary, I think most farmers appreciate the "strong, virile and sexy" stereotype now. Of course, we have to be aware of the power of the advertisers and how they could change it and therefore, influence opinion. For now though, farmers are "in" so you just have to look at those advertisements and model yourself on them to be seen as a good catch!

Indeed, as farmers are being viewed as desirable by some sectors of society, a recent newspaper article joked (perhaps with a nugget of truth) that cattle farmers are "being eyed up as 'trophy husband' material by young women with large salaries wishing to marry into a supposedly idyllic rural lifestyle."[46]

THE ATTRACTIVENESS OF A FARMER

Almost without realising it, you already stand out from those townie competitors, but you must ensure it is in a positive way! Remember, some women may be determined never to marry a farmer, even if they were brought up on a farm. But you have all this going for you:

◢ Farmers have to be physically strong to be able to carry newborn calves, catch cattle's heads to dose them, lift heavy tractor parts and more. Being able to carry a very heavy object seemingly effortlessly is going to look very sexy. Remember it has to look easy in order to impress. It'll be even more remarkable if she tried to lift it first and couldn't even budge it. If you can swing a 10-stone bag of meal over your shoulder and carry it to the livestock, you'll have no problem carrying her over a muddy gap.

◢ You look healthy and tanned. Okay, she may not have had the pleasure yet of seeing a farmer naked and discovering that his skin is milk-bottle white under his clothes, but your general fitness and bronzed arms will impress.

◢ Bringing a newborn animal into the world can be a very special and bonding moment. Have a towel handy to rub down the cute lambs as all that gunk might put her off, but once the lamb or calf is walking around on shaky legs, that's when it's going to feel a very special moment.

⌐ Having your own business means you are your own man and, therefore, sexy. You may be broke but you carry respect. Being self-employed might suggest you can work whatever hours you want and take holidays at the best times of the year.

⌐ Farmers can almost multi-task in that they are extremely adaptable and can turn their hands to almost anything from a fixing a tractor to putting up a shelf to unblocking a sink to working out why the dog is limping. They can also fix almost anything with baler twine – guaranteed. Maybe not a broken leg but certainly anything else.

⌐ Family means a lot to farmers. Most farms have been in the family for generations and farmers have grown up with extended family visiting or living on the farm. They drive him mad at times but he's loyal and they mean a lot to him. This suggests you'd be faithful to your girlfriend too.

⌐ If you have lots of land, you are seen as a good catch. Yes, that's right, it's the good old road frontage.

WHERE TO GO ON A FIRST DATE

The first date is the most important. If it doesn't go well, there won't be a second one. Where should you bring her to ensure you both have a great time and get to know each other without there being too many awkward silences?

A posh restaurant

Going to a very posh restaurant might be tough going if there are gaps in the conversation and there are just the two of you. Of course you can do posh, but if nerves makes you forget which cutlery to use and you're concentrating on that instead of your date, it's going to create unwanted tension.

There won't be a big mug of tea at the end of the meal either, just a tiny cup of coffee – it would be best not to grumble about that.

A walk on the beach

She will think you're being romantic suggesting a stroll along by the seafront while really you're checking if she's good for a long walk. Gaps in the conversation are never awkward when you're strolling along as you're soaking in the beauty of the scene. You'll get extra marks for offering her your jacket if it gets chilly.

To the cinema

Perfect. There's plenty of scope to chat even if it's just about the movie. As long as you don't snore, you might even catch up on forty winks half way through the film if you've been suffering sleep deprivation or have been up since 4am.

A hill walk and a picnic

If the weather is good, pack up a nice picnic and head for the hills for a long walk and some amazing scenery. Another way to find out if she's fit and strong! But if your mother packed the picnic for you, it would be best to keep this to yourself.

A Young Farmers club

Okay, I know you want to show her what your life is all about and your deep love for farming but unless she's a member of this club too, will she really be impressed? You don't want to frighten her off by introducing her to your friends on a first date, particularly if the main topic of conversation is who has cut their silage already or how the rain is affecting crop yields.

And, looking to the future, when you do take her to the club, tell her in advance where you're going in case she arrives in a skimpy top and stilettos – she just might feel out of place among check shirts, jeans and boots.

Pub with friends

Meeting two or four friends at the pub should be a good evening if you're both comfortable meeting new people. Not too many to be overwhelming and yet enough to keep the conversation flowing.

Tips for a successful first date

⌐ Do not bring the farm jeep to pick her up. Borrow a car if necessary. You may not notice it but the jeep probably smells of that dead calf you brought to the vet lab last week, your mucky wellies and the air freshener you hung up to try and mask the other smells. And those stains – what *are* they?

⌐ Just as you will never reveal the number of acres owned, don't expect her to tell you about her assets. Do not ask her about her salary or if she happens to own any land. If your relationship does continue, she will always wonder if you're more interested in the land, the pay packet or her.

⌐ Do not go Dutch on a first date. Farmers have a bad enough reputation for being stingy as it is. Play your part in shelving that stereotype.

⌐ Do not talk about ex-girlfriends nor refer to the fact that they dumped you because of your mother or the amount of attention you give to your cows.

⌐ While you can discuss favourite foods, don't attempt to suss out if she can cook a slap-up meal for up to ten contractors.

⌐ If she is vegetarian or vegan, don't mention getting your pet lambs slaughtered for the freezer.

⌐ If she decides against having a dessert but then asks for a second spoon when yours arrives, don't begrudge her half of it. She probably just changed her mind when she saw how lovely it looked, but it is also a good test of whether you are generous and kind or evil, mean-spirited and selfish. No woman wants a man who won't share dessert or chocolate with her.

⅃ Complaining that you're hungry after a restaurant meal and insisting on stopping for chips isn't necessarily a good idea. She'll be wondering if you're going to be really fat in ten years' time.

#NeverDo

For a second date, one farmer used to phone his new girlfriend to say he was running late and ask her to meet him at the farm. When she arrived, he asked for some help with something relatively easy like stopping a gap or moving a cow from one shed to another. If she helped, there was a third date. If she flounced off or was unable to help, he knew she wasn't right for his lifestyle. I never found out if he ever married.

MEETING THE FAMILY

A few dates have gone by without a hitch and you are thinking this relationship might become long term. It's meet the family time. Having a farm adds another layer of complication to the usual introductions. Not only do you have to meet her family and she yours, but you want to showcase your family farm as a place she might want to live one day. You want to prove that living on this farm is the best place in the world to live.

I met Brian's extended family for the first time at his nephew's christening. Having purchased a new dress for the occasion, I never thought of bringing farming clothes with me. Brian, as the uncle and the student, had the job of milking the cows that evening and seemed to think I'd be happy enough chatting to his various relations while he was working. I remember chasing after him and insisting he find me a pair of wellies. I had no problem with going for the cows and milking in my new dress and borrowed wellies, but he also got me a pair of his jeans, a belt and a shirt. I'm not sure if the relatives thought I was an antisocial introvert or a hard worker!

Introducing her to your farm

You may have heard horror stories of other farmers' girlfriends running a mile when they saw the farm and are perhaps thinking it would be better to keep her away for as long as possible, maybe even until after you have proposed and she has said yes.

If you try to dissuade her from visiting the farm, she will wonder if you're hiding something, if there's something suspicious about your family or if you're ashamed of her.

Don't be afraid to bring her home to the farm but you do need to prepare first, especially if she's not from farming stock. Remember that she might judge the farm from what she has seen on television so you might be compared to the pristine farms on *Countryfile* or *Ear to the Ground*.

What might put her off?

- Mud – lots and lots of muck. Don't bring her when it's been pouring with rain for two weeks. Let it dry off for a few days and give the yard a good wash with the power washer.

- An untidy yard. If there's rusty old machinery lying around, gutters and gates falling down and piles of waste plastic around the place, you need to have a good tidy up. She'll wonder if there will ever be a chance of a nice tidy house and garden.

- Country smells. It would be best not to invite her when there is slurry being agitated or spread. Your dad smelling of "eau de slurrai" at the table isn't going to endear her to country life if she's not already used to it. Let her visit on a "cutting silage" day when the air is filled with the sweet scent of grass (but check first if she has hay fever, in which case it might be prudent to postpone it for a fortnight).

⌐ Feeding the contractors. This is a tricky one. If she calls on the day the silage is brought in and your mum is cooking for eight hungry workers, she might view it as wonderful that wholesome food is so heartily appreciated ... or she might baulk and run.

⌐ Lots of family. It's good to show that family is important to you but don't let her first visit be a family occasion when all your mad (there will be some, even if you can't see it) relatives are in attendance. What the family views as just Auntie Mavis's way and Uncle Frank's mild eccentricity, might lead her to wonder who else you have locked in the attic and whether the eccentricity is hereditary. Besides which, she will have similar family members who she's trying to get away from! There's always a black sheep somewhere in the family! Plus, a lot of family at one go can be a tad overwhelming. Remember never to judge each other by your relatives.

⌐ Noise. She might be dreaming of birdsong and tranquillity, but because of that small wood near the yard all she can hear is the cawing of crows above the clatter of machinery. Yes, that's going to be the way it is sometimes, but let her see (hear) that there is peace to be had too.

The black sheep in the family.

The one person in the family who is different from all the others; not at all reputable and possibly a source of shame.

What will warm the cockles of her heart?

⌐ Invite her to help with the herding and ensure they are grazing fields with the best views.

⌐ Bring her for a ride on the quad (clean it first) so she can wrap her arms tightly around you.

- Show her around the yard and farm that is so much a part of your life. If she hasn't got wellington boots, don't expect her to cram her feet into your mum's old ones. Buy her a pair as a welcoming gift. It's not quite like giving her the key to your apartment, but it is a perfect way to indicate you are inviting her into your life.

- Invite her to help you bring in the cows, making sure to walk them home the scenic route (preferably along by the hedges with the honeysuckle so it smells and looks idyllic).

- Bring her to spread some fertiliser with you some evening. Remember to check the passenger seat is comfortable (bring a cushion if not), the tractor reasonably clean and don't drive too fast over bumpy ground. Admire the deep red sunset and watch the sun go down, feeling like you're the only two people in the whole world.

- Let her bottle feed a young lamb or calf, but give her one that's easy to feed. A stubborn calf can make someone feel that there must be an easier life than that of a dairy farmer!

- Ask for her help to dig the spuds! If she's into sustainable living, pulling carrots and picking raspberries before cooking dinner together sends so many great messages. All supposing, of course, that you don't have to ask your mam where the veg patch is or how to turn on the oven.

How best to introduce her to the mother?

#NeverDo
Don't invite her to dinner if she is vegetarian. Your mother won't know what to cook and your father will keep mentioning the benefits of rare steak. Invite her for afternoon tea and scones instead.

Much depends on your mother's opinion of you so you need to recognise and acknowledge exactly what it is first. We all know that farming sons are the apple of their mother's eye but ...

 Are you her golden boy?

 Does she expect you to be looked after in the way in which you are accustomed?

 Does she see you at being at risk of being snapped up by a gold-digger who is only after you for half the farm and the road frontage?

 Is she suspicious of the attention that you give others?

 Is she the main decision-maker on the farm at the moment? Is she going to want to maintain that power?

Or:

 Has she raised you to be capable of making up your own mind?

 Does she know you are a good judge of character?

 Is she so desperate for cute grandchildren (perhaps an heir and a spare) that she will welcome any lady to the farm?

 Does she want nothing more than to see you happy, in love and loved?

 Is she looking forward to having another woman on the farm?

Depending on which criteria you've said yes to, the amount of preparation could be quite significant. But whatever the situation, **if any of the following apply to your girlfriend, your mother needs to know about them:**

ð Farmers in her extended family (but not that she just visited them once a year on a Sunday afternoon).

ð Priests or vicars in the family.

ð Celebrity relations (unless they are known drug addicts).

- ☸ Awards, even if it was just winning the 100m at school (being able to sprint is a welcome skill on a livestock farm) or getting a prize for her scones in the local county show.

- ☸ Ownership of a house or apartment (to dispel fears of gold-digging).

- ☸ A tasty-looking car. (We're talking here of the type that would impress the neighbours.)

- ☸ Qualifications and career choice. Financially independent with the capability to be a laying hen.

She will be relaying all the positives to her friends and neighbours so give her plenty to work with.

Remember: Your mother's opinion of your girlfriend will differ according to who she is talking to. If your girlfriend isn't from a farming background, your mother may criticise her to her best friend as she wonders if she will adjust to the farming life. She may consider her wellies to be too flowery and her skirt too long/short to be practical on the farm. Perhaps your girlfriend didn't eat many scones so she must be on a permanent diet and how will she keep you fed and happy at all?

However, to everyone else, she will sing her praises. She will emphasise her good job, her qualifications, her parentage, her nice car, how she is taking to some farming jobs like a duck to water, and how she brought the most delicious home-made cake the last time she visited. Your mother may have fed half the cake to the hens the following day but as far as the neighbours are concerned, it was utterly delightful.

A laying hen.

A woman who works outside the farm to bring in a regular income but is also able to help out on the farm during her time off.

What to tell your girlfriend

Your girlfriend could be imagining all kinds of farm-wife-type stereotypes. She might visualise your mother as a plump yet fit and hard-working farmer's wife who wears a wrap-around apron, milks cows, makes cheese, bakes bread, grows vegetables and arranges flowers at the drop of a hat. If your mother is a stick thin, suit-wearing accountant who doesn't know where the tractor is parked, doesn't possess an Aga and her only contact with sheep is when she puts a leg of lamb in the oven, let your girlfriend know.

Tell her your mother's hobbies so she knows to talk about areas of common interest (e.g. education, travel, books, television programmes, gardening). She can get into her good books by asking for advice on growing delphiniums or requesting your mum's recipe for brown bread.

If she wants to bring a gift, help her out with some ideas. She won't want to bring a bottle of wine if your parents don't drink alcohol, or a box of chocolates if your dad is a diabetic and your mum is on a permanent diet (even if it is a "see-food diet").

How to impress her family

You'll want to make an impression (a good one). All boyfriends have this to face, but it may be just a tad more challenging for farmers. So:

- When you're getting ready, empty the hot-water tank by scrubbing away any lingering slurry smells or splashes of muck. Use a scrubbing brush on your fingernails.
- Use a small amount of faintly scented aftershave.
- Dress smartly but unless you're going to a very smart restaurant, keep it casual.

◢ Don't be late.

◢ Read the papers for the week beforehand so you are up to date on national and international news. You'll have already read the farming papers of course, so if your girlfriend is from a farming family, you'll be on safe ground.

◢ Stay away from the topics of religion and politics. However, check if they say grace before the meal in case you start tucking in without realising. (It goes without saying that you should stay away from the topic of sex – *in any form whatsoever*.)

◢ If your only vehicle is the farm jeep, borrow your parents' car, or your friend's, or anyone's, so long as it doesn't have mud splatters over it and looks like a mobile engineer's workshop inside.

◢ Bring flowers or a box of chocolates for her mother and a decent bottle of wine for her father. Whatever about her father, make sure you get into the mother's good books.

◢ Admire the garden (unless there are lots of obvious weeds).

◢ Ask your girlfriend beforehand if there are any family feuds or divorces just in case you put a large foot in it by asking about a relative and there's a frosty silence.

◢ Leave your mobile phone switched off.

◢ Do not drink more than one glass of wine or one glass of beer. Your similarly inebriated mates may think you're great craic after ten pints on a Friday night but your future mother-in-law won't. Take that on trust.

◢ Help to clear the table. Remember you need to impress her mother.

◢ Don't fall asleep after dinner.

◢ If you can, tell stories of family bliss and an idyllic childhood (so they can picture that for their grandchildren).

◢ Do not curse or swear. No, really. Remember this is a first meeting. Whatever they say, *it is a test*.

◢ Don't tell stories of exaggerated near-death experiences on the farm that will make them fear their daughter will be a young widow.

◢ If they are from the city, emphasise your education, just in case they think you're a modern version of the *Beverly Hillbillies*.

Once you've both endured and survived the first meeting with the opposite family and assuming neither of you has been put off, you've passed the main hurdles. It's up to both of you to decide if you're going to take it further. This quiz should help!

FARM COUPLE QUIZ

For him: Is she right for you?

		Yes	No
1.	Does she make you laugh?	❏	❏
2.	Can she take long walking strides across the fields and keep up with you?	❏	❏
3.	Can she drive a tractor, shear a sheep or at least know one end of a cow from the other?	❏	❏
4.	Does she enjoy taking photographs of your cows and sheep for her Instagram account?	❏	❏
5.	Does she go for the cows with you and see it as a nice relaxing stroll?	❏	❏
6.	Can she stand in a gap?	❏	❏
7.	Does she understand what you mean when you say "pass me that yoke"?	❏	❏
8.	Does she laugh when your new pup jumps up on her?	❏	❏

9. Is she happy to drive while you navigate (and peer over the hedges into the fields)? ❑ ❑

10. Does she always have a pair of old shoes or wellies in the car – just in case? ❑ ❑

Score out of 10 for Yes

8–10 Perfect, you're a match made in Heaven.

5–7 It's not her fault: you need to work on your vocabulary (how is she expected to know what a yoke is?), and take shorter strides.

1–4 Okay, you may need to buy her a copy of *How To Be A Perfect Farm Wife* and then take the test again when she's read it.

For her: Is he shaping up to be an Ideal Farm Husband?

Yes No

1. Does he teach you how to do something on the farm and then it's your job whenever you are there? ❑ ❑

2. Does he love to sit in the passenger seat and give you a running commentary on what is in the fields as you drive past? ❑ ❑

3. Has he said "My mother never ..." or "My mother always makes it with xxx" within your hearing? ❑ ❑

4. Does he forget to hold the door open for you when you're going to a restaurant or another venue? ❑ ❑

5. Did he use a chat up line like "Have you much in the way of road frontage?" or "You look in fine fettle; I'd say you like your spuds"? ❏ ❏

6. When requesting that you bring lunch or tea to him in the Buttercup Field, did he forget to provide you with a map with the field names clearly marked on it? ❏ ❏

7. Does he swear when you're helping him sort livestock and "the wrong one" gets past you? ❏ ❏

8. Does he neglect to clean out the farm jeep/car at least annually? ❏ ❏

9. Does he forget to remind you that you'll need wellies when inviting you for a romantic walk across the fields in the summer? ❏ ❏

10. Did he serve up a (cold but reheated) takeaway when he invited you to a dinner at the farm for just the two of you? ❏ ❏

Score out of 10 for Yes

8–10 Eeek, okay, take a deep breath, it doesn't look good but answer the questions again when he's finished reading this book and has put the tips into practice.

5–7 He's showing promise; with a bit of work, he'll get there soon.

1–4 His mother trained him very well. Buy her a bunch of flowers right now.

PART FIVE

YOUR PRE-MARRIAGE COURSE

HOW TO PROPOSE

You've decided she is the one for you. For better or for worse, you want to spend the rest of your life with her. Never mind these days of enlightenment, the marriage proposal is still most likely going to have to come from you. And popping the question is a big moment: you want her to say yes and at the same time you want it to be memorable and special.

So what's the best way to go about it? Maybe this is good news for you, but it seems bringing her to a romantic destination like Paris or New York is quite passé now. Forget the top of the Eiffel Tower and think bales or ploughing. Yes, there's going to be the three of you in this marriage: You, Her and (Wait! No, not your mother), the Farm! Therefore, it makes sense if the farm is there for the proposal too, doesn't it?

Proposing with impact takes some planning but can be done. First, though: will she appreciate the grand gesture, or will it mortify her? Admittedly you need to be the type of person who doesn't care what the neighbours say.

If you think it's safe to proceed, start organising. You should have most requirements to hand apart from the helicopter. Don't stop reading! The helicopter is optional. These are all tried and tested ways of asking that all-important question.

Wrapped bales and paint

Line up wrapped silage bales in a field and paint one letter on each bale to spell out "Will You Marry Me?", not forgetting to add her name of course. It will have to be the time of year when bales are in the field and you can arrange them in a long line. You just need to buy a paintbrush and paint in a colour that will stand out.

Consider the placement of the wrapped bales carefully. Do you want them near a busy road where other people might see them before she does (especially if, horror of horrors, she says no)? Can you place them in a field that isn't overlooked by traffic and yet you can stroll to a nice scenic spot from where to view the proposal?

A plough and ~~the stars~~
No, a field

Planning to plough a field? Before you plough the complete acreage, follow the example of Scottish farm worker John Jardine and plough the words "Will You Marry Me?" into the grass. He brought his girlfriend to a castle on a nearby hill from where to view it.[47] The castle is a nice touch, but if you are lacking such a structure, you need a field at the foot of a steep hill, or a helicopter!

A field and spray

A farmer from Milton Keynes used a quad to spray the proposal into a crop so the plants died and the letters showed up.[48] If she's frugal, she's going to baulk at the fact that you're losing money on your crop. Don't even think of going there if she's into organic farming.

If you're shaking your head at the thought of this method, I'm totally with you – I couldn't countenance it either. Maybe if you're going to reseed grass, spray the words before you spray the entire field? Remember you need to get your certificate in the use of sprays and sprayer operation first!

A field and manure!

Yes, you read that right – manure! An American farmer used a slurry spreader to spray "Will You Marry Me?" on to his freshly harvested alfalfa field so the brown stood out nicely against the very pale green. He brought his girlfriend up in a helicopter to view it. Spraying the slurry neatly so it forms letters would be some challenge! (As would getting hold of a helicopter, I imagine.) Obviously you'd have to view this one from some distance away, so make those letters large!

Rolling in the hay

If you make straw or hay bales, this could be a good option. An Australian farmer spent a couple of hours arranging numerous hay bales into the words "Will You Marry Me?" and brought his girlfriend up in a helicopter to view it.[49]

Branches

Another proposal method is using branches from fallen trees. You can shape the letters and either fix them into the ground so they stand up and are visible to you when standing (and you are lacking that all-important helicopter), or lay them out on the ground if the proposal can be viewed from a height. Brown branches against a snowy hill would look very effective too (as long as you get there before it snows again and the branches get covered!).

A mature tree and a penknife

This probably wouldn't be so good for the tree but there's something timeless and romantic about carving into bark. Have you got a wood on your farm or a particularly spectacular old tree? Carve the proposal into the bark and bring her for a walk and a picnic at the foot of the tree.

Romantic picnic

For all of these "outdoor" proposal venues, remember to bring a picnic with you for that romantic touch. You don't even have to make it all yourself. You can contact a "picnic business" and they will provide you with the elegant picnic basket, the champagne, the wine glasses, the food and of course, the rug – everything you need for making that moment extra special.

Stay clear of the field where the slurry is spread though! Also, getting your mam to pack the picnic is a bit of a no-no.

An agricultural show and a prize-winning cow

If you have the courage to propose in public, an agricultural show is a great place and, of course, you'll get to go back every year and relive the memories. So, how can you do it with style in a way that will not only compel her to say yes but will also make her the envy of every farmer's girlfriend and wife?

Follow Alex Burrows' example and when showing a large animal (he had a prize-winning cow), slip the banner embroidered with "Will You Marry Me?" onto the animal just before you walk in for the grand parade.[50] All eyes will turn to her in the auditorium – just make sure she is sitting there watching and hasn't nipped off to the loo.

Book and champagne

If the other methods sound overly complicated and your motto in life is to keep things simple and straightforward, but you still want to be romantic and make it memorable, present her with a copy of *Would You Marry A Farmer?* and of course, bring along the champagne. Much easier, and she'll enjoy reading the book too!

As an aside, there's a farm diversification idea in this. As these methods of proposals are becoming so popular, city slickers are hiring farmers to provide their field and mow or plough the words for them.[51]

A cash cow.

A source of regular and dependable income.

SHOULD YOU BUY THE RING IN ADVANCE?

Brian proposed to me out of the blue. I think he almost surprised himself. We'd had a difference of opinion on the phone and he hopped in his car to come and see me. As he was living 50 miles away, he had plenty of time to decide whether he wanted to throttle me or marry me. So he didn't have time to think about a ring. I wouldn't have had a notion what I wanted; I'd never even considered whether I preferred yellow gold or white gold, or a solitaire diamond or a cluster.

Not all women want the same thing. Some women would prefer to choose their own ring; some would prefer their partner to put time and thought into selecting it carefully; others want to shop for the ring together.

Whether or not to buy the ring in advance is a difficult decision unless you are very sure of your ground. Maybe these arguments for and against will help you decide.

Why you might buy the ring in advance:
- ♂ She loves you so much that she will love anything you pick and she has complete faith in your taste in jewellery. You know she has genuinely loved everything you've bought her so far.

○ A few of her friends have got engaged recently and she's mentioned the ring, so you've got a good idea what she likes and doesn't like so you're feeling confident.

○ She knows you detest shopping, so if you spend a whole morning picking out a ring, she's going to know just how much you love her.

○ You know she wouldn't like to know what it cost and she wouldn't like you to go over what you can afford either.

○ You believe that if you can't choose a ring for her, how can you spend the rest of your lives together, making decisions?

○ You don't want her to know how much it cost. (That is not an excuse to buy a cheap ring by the way!)

○ It will make the proposal all the more romantic if you can present her with the ring.

Tip: Always check with the jeweller that you can exchange it. Just in case.

Why not to buy the ring in advance:
○ Hollywood films and romantic fiction always have the heroine loving the ring he picked out and it always fits perfectly, but real life may not work out like that for you.

○ You don't want to run the risk of her turning you down because she doesn't like the ring.

○ You might think three diamonds in a row is fabulous but if she would prefer a solitaire diamond or a sapphire, she is going to be disappointed.

○ She might have admired rings in the past and you think you know just what she likes. She loves it in the box but when she tries it on, it just doesn't suit her hand.

○ You haven't a clue what she likes and they all look much the same to you. You're going to bow to her expertise and just produce yourself and the wallet.

○ As she is going to be wearing it for many years, it has to be right. No pressure!

If you wish to offer her a ring (but not the real deal) during the proposal, make it fun by welding a small bolt to a washer (just like farmer Andrew Gallon in Northumberland did,[52] sensible man) or produce a jubilee clip so she can wear that in the interim and even hold on to as a keepsake. I'm presuming she will know you well enough to know you aren't that tight with money and she'll recognise the jubilee clip is symbolic – if there is a chance she's not going to be sure, you may want to rethink this whole thing.

Whatever you do, don't hand her a sum of money and send her off to buy her engagement ring on her own or with a friend. That is *not* romantic, and suppose the ring she wants is a couple of hundred euro/pounds/dollars more than you gave her? Do you really want her to have to put her own money to it or get a less expensive ring? My advice is to start married life the way it will always be and just go over budget on her gifts. She might look more kindly on the fact that you buy a newer or bigger tractor than you intended when you go machinery shopping.

Buying the ring together should be a special time, so after shopping for the ring, go for a really nice afternoon tea in a good hotel. This might be the one and only time in your life that you will eat tiny crustless sandwiches and you'll consider each one to be a mere extravagant bite, but be indulgent. And, just a tip here, don't moan about the price or say that your mam would be horrified or that you'd prefer a doorstep ham and cheese sarnie.

PRE-NUPTIAL AGREEMENTS: THE GOOD, THE BAD AND THE UGLY

Divorce wasn't possible in Ireland until 1996 so the issues of maintenance and settlements have become significant issues only in the last 20 years. It took a long time for divorce to be passed, partly because so many in the farming community were fearful of what would happen to the family farm in this situation. The Irish courts received 55,000 applications for separations and divorce between 2000 and 2010. Before 1996, it was a case of "you made your bed, now you have to lie on it".

Therefore, farmers didn't have to consider the repercussions of a break-up too seriously before 1996, at least in financial terms. However, if they broke off an engagement in the mid twentieth century, it was a different story. Irish newspapers carry reports of farmers being brought to court for a breach of promise of marriage and ordered to pay compensation to their once-intended bride.

A cook was awarded £150 in 1932 as her intended, a farmer, ended the relationship three days before the wedding. She was 47 and had left her job as a cook where she earned £52 a year, plus she had spent £30 preparing for the wedding.[53]

In 1953, a farmer's daughter was awarded £600 in damages in her breach of promise action against a farmer. They had agreed in 1944 to marry. She had a baby in 1951 and he promised marriage within a reasonable time (so one would assume he was the father). However, in court, he denied the promise and said that if he had made it, it was because he believed her to be chaste and modest! Two other men proposed to her "in the early days" and were refused. It might have influenced the judge that she had given up other chances of marriage. £600 was a significant sum, enough to purchase a farm and, of course, she had a child so her reputation was damaged. Plus he had kept her waiting for almost ten years![54]

What is a pre-nuptial agreement?

It is a contract between two people who are going to marry, stating how their assets will be divided should the relationship come to an end. For a wedding involving a farmer, it is usually put in place to protect the land. However, while a working spouse may not have much capital at the time of marriage, she may have a considerable pension in the future that she might want to protect. It deals with issues such as the division of present and future property, maintenance payments, pensions, indemnity for debt and separation costs.

Should you have a pre-nup?

Apparently seven out of ten Irish farmers are now in favour of pre-nuptial agreements.[55] Even though it looks like the present government will not be proceeding to give pre-nuptials legal standing in Ireland, media reports suggest the courts may take them into consideration in the case of a settlement as long as children and spouses are provided for properly.[56] Stories of divorces after a couple of years of marriage and "the young wan" leaving the relationship with half a farm tend to dominate when discussion of marriage and pre-nuptials comes up. However, the reality is that when half the farm goes to a spouse, it's usually after 30 or 40 years of marriage. Yes, divorce happens to older married couples too.

Although one of every six pieces of land put up for sale is because of a relationship breakdown,[57] it seems that tales of half a farm being sold to fund a divorce are usually myths. Circumstances vary, but in a recent Supreme Court ruling the spouse was awarded 25% of an inherited farm.[58] That's not to say that a farmer won't have to sell off a considerable portion of land to fund a settlement. Most Irish farmers are hugely attached to their land, yet a judge can be quick to part a farmer from his sentiments if the farm isn't a viable business and there are no other assets to fund maintenance in a divorce.[59]

If the non-farming spouse isn't working and is looking after young children, a home and maintenance payments will be required from the farmer. If she paid a substantial deposit on the marital home (usually located on the farm), invested money and worked on the farm, gave up work to be the main childcarer, I think most would agree she deserves a payout from the business. However, farms tend to be asset rich and cash poor so the settlement is usually funded through the sale of an asset.

It's not very romantic is it? Ireland has a heritage of marriages being arranged for financial and business reasons, often to provide a family to carry on the farm as well as increase its size, scope and success. In those cases it could be seen as part of the business deal. Maybe it's the romantic films of Hollywood or maybe a backlash to the olden ways of doing things, but many view a pre-nuptial agreement as too business-like in a relationship built on love and trust.

But is it advisable to get one to protect the farm from being split or sold off? Or would getting one risk your relationship? Would you both be entering into marriage wondering if you're just waiting for failure? Let's look at it from different perspectives.

Why the farmer's parents might want pre-nuptials in place

The farm has been in the family for generations, they have farmed it themselves for many decades. They don't see it as just an asset or a business to be handed over to a child. There are memories and stories and family histories tied up in those fields, they attach significant sentiment to their farm.

There's also the worry that the farm won't be a viable business if part of it has to be sold off. Would it herald the end of the farm?

They might be afraid a "gold-digging hussy" will take half the farm in a divorce just a couple of years after marriage. Even worse, she might have married him to get half the farm. They want to ensure that the relationship will last before they hand over the farm.

They might want the new daughter-in-law to prove that she's marrying their son for love, not to take half of what they have sacrificed. They might even be expecting the daughter-in-law to bring a substantial sum with her or a gift from her parents (yes, some do, even these days).

If a pre-nuptial is not forthcoming, parents have been known to delay handing over the farm to their child, which can create all kinds of problems. He isn't in a position to get bank loans to invest or make decisions for the future of the farm, which can lead to frustration, anger and ineptitude. This could also mean that the daughter-in-law has no security whatsoever if her husband were to die, which could have serious implications if they have young children. It wasn't unheard of, in the past, for a childless young widow to be sent back to her family with nothing but the dowry she had brought with her.

Why a farmer might want a pre-nuptial

Because his parents won't hand over the farm or form a legal partnership until there is a pre-nuptial agreement in place.

Because he owns the farm and has heard stories of others losing theirs and is determined it's not going to happen to him. He's not necessarily being selfish but he feels beholden to his parents and previous generations. He is a custodian of the farm and believes it is his responsibility to improve it and hand it on to the next generation.

How your girlfriend might feel on being asked for a pre-nuptial

- ŏ That she's being treated like a gold-digger when her only thought is that she loves you.

- ŏ Insulted to be asked, believing she is seen as suspicious rather than trustworthy.

- ŏ That you are going into marriage expecting it to fail at some point, or at least your parents do.

- ŏ Annoyed that her input into the farm isn't necessarily going to be taken into consideration.

- ŏ That you are bowing to pressure from your parents, which won't help her relationship with them, and she'll wonder if you will always be influenced by them.

- ŏ That the wedding vows of "for richer, for poorer" might not mean that you are going to work together for success.

- ŏ Understanding that the farm has been in the family for generations and she wouldn't want to see it split either, so she is happy to make the agreement; besides, she doesn't expect it ever to come to that.

☿ Independent and secure in a well-paid job with a pension so she doesn't see that she would ever need the farm, especially if her annual income is greater than yours.

☿ That it protects her assets too: her income and her future pension.

☿ Happy to have the subject of finances out in the open and you can plan for different circumstances that might arise when you get married.

As you can see, just bringing up the pre-nuptial could be a very sticky subject and the discussion should really be between the couple themselves without any interference from parents.

Would I expect my son or daughter (if one of them takes over the farm) to sign a pre-nuptial agreement with a partner?

I'm 47 (aaagh, feeling old) and our children are 12 and 14. It might be a very different situation if the child to inherit was 20 now and wanted to get married within a decade. Brian and I would be in our mid-50s; we've invested heavily in the farm and have worked extremely hard to make bank repayments and most of the loans would have just come to an end. Would the farm be able to support two family incomes? Would I resent the fact that our pensions aren't as big as I'd like them to be because we invested so much in the farm? Would I feel we were just starting to enjoy the fruits of our labours not to mention having a bit of spare cash at last? Would I be anxious about the future break-up of the farm?

As the situation stands, I'd say we will be on our knees by the time one of the children has finished university, travelled, worked in the rat race for a while to get it out of their system and then decided to come back to farm. Would I want them to sign a pre-nuptial? I wouldn't want anything to do with that decision, it would be between them. I can't take the land with me and although I'd like my ashes to be scattered on my favourite field sometime, it wouldn't really matter if they weren't.

I think it is really important the older couple have sufficient money invested for their pension so they don't need an income from the farm on retiring. Ideally, they should feel they have given the farm what they can and got what they deserved from it (a good lifestyle, a sense of achievement, some creature comforts and some holidays) and are happy to pass it on with all the luck in the world to their child. We can't control the future and even if the worst were to happen, people can usually find it within themselves to pick themselves up again. We can't bring our farms into the coffins with us, although I think many would if they could!

When chickens come home to roost.

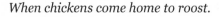 When the consequences of actions in the past catch up with you, but in a bad way. It comes from the proverb: Curses, like chickens, come home to roost.

WHAT IF SHE DOESN'T WANT TO TAKE YOUR NAME?

The family name is very important in farming. It can even be a factor in why sons are favoured over daughters in terms of inheritance. Just as a father "gave away" his daughter to the man she was marrying, traditionally the woman took her husband's name on marriage.

More women are keeping their own surname now, or are considering it carefully before they decide to give it up. Some keep their own name for their work and as children come along, they slowly start using their husband's name. It's rare that a man takes his wife's name, but it does happen.

Brian and I were engaged for two months before the name change even occurred to me. I remember I was horrified. I'd had my name for almost 23 years, I couldn't give it up just like that. I remember thinking aloud and saying "Look, we can't get married; I really don't want to be Mrs James". Although the wedding was in six months' time, I was prepared to postpone it until I could get used to the idea of the name change. Our best man came up with a solution; he suggested that I sandwich both names together. I did, but I used Sixsmith-James only for a couple of years. It's on my passport, driving licence and bank accounts but it's too much of a mouthful.

I'm occasionally called Mrs James if someone connected to the children contacts me, but most people know me as my own name. As our farm has been known as Sixsmiths for over a century, it creates confusion at times. As Brian's surname is also used as a popular first name, he gets called lots of different variations such as Brian Sixsmith, James Sixsmith, James Bryan, and James O'Brien. Just as when people get my name wrong occasionally, sometimes we correct them; sometimes we just smile and nod.

Don't be affronted if your girlfriend decides to keep her own name. It's not because she doesn't want the hassle of having to change it back if you divorce. It's not because she doesn't like your name. It's probably not because there are no boys in her family to carry on the name. Reasons differ. For me, it was about who I was and wanting to stay as that person. I also think it might have had something to do with my grandmother and great aunts. As I was curled up in an armchair on Sunday afternoons reading my Enid Blyton books and they were catching up on news, I'd hear them refer to someone by her maiden name to explain who she was. I think, from an early age, I never wanted old women to refer to me as "She used to be a Sixsmith". We have been married for 24 years and I still can't imagine being called anything other than Lorna Sixsmith, but it doesn't mean that I love Brian or the children any less. And as I do occasional interviews about farming and my books, the children are often relieved they have a different surname to me!

Of course, if you prefer not to have different surnames, you could take each other's names and go double-barrelled. If that's too much of a mouthful, create a whole new surname! We could have become "Sixjames"!

PLANNING YOUR LIVING ARRANGEMENTS

Where to live

Where are you going to live when you get married or move in together? This isn't a trick question. Your decision could impact on your relationship with each other and with the rest of your family.

What tend to be the choices?

Build a house for yourselves on the farm

✔ You have your own home close to the farmyard which makes life much easier, especially during the calving/lambing seasons.

✔ It makes a huge difference to family life as you can pop in for a quick cuppa if you need a break and see the kids or if you need to look after them for half an hour. It's easier too for the rest of the family to take a stroll up the yard to collect eggs or bring in the cows. You all see more of each other for very little effort.

✘ If both houses are close to the farmyard, you could be limiting the value of the second one as it's unlikely it could ever be sold separate to the farm.

✘ Your house might be too close to your parents' for each house to have a reasonable amount of privacy.

✘ If you build it some distance from the farmyard, it's quite a trek in the middle of the night when a cow is calving or when the children just want to go and collect the eggs.

Build a bungalow for your parents and you move into the farmhouse

✔ Your mum would probably love a new house with a brand new kitchen.

✔ Your parents might be getting to the age where having all the rooms on the ground floor will be an advantage.

✔ There can be some distance between the two houses so each has privacy.

✘ Depending on your budget, your wife may have to live with your mother's taste in decor for some time.

✘ Your parents might be upset if you change the decor and rip out the kitchen and bathrooms. You may hear comments like "that hall carpet was almost brand new, it had years of use left in it" or "those new tiles make the kitchen very cold".

Rent or buy a house in the nearest town and live there

✔ If your wife is from a large city and is hesitant about the move to the farm, this might be a good half way situation for the first year or two as she acclimatises to rural life.

✘ Unless it's only a mile or so to the farm, it would be a nightmare for you long term. It would be difficult to have a good family life as your hours are not 9–5 and it could get quite lonely on the farm during long days.

✘ If you have children, it would be difficult for them to spend time with you.

✘ If your girlfriend doesn't want to live on or visit the farm, it's going to be hard on your relationship.

We did this for the first three years when we returned to farming. It helped me to adjust to small town community living but wasn't so easy for Brian having to commute. Life became much more straightforward when we moved to the farm.

Rent a house near the farm

✔ Renting gives you privacy.

✔ If your girlfriend is from the town, it gives her time to adjust to country life without being in the middle of the farm.

✔ As you are spending money on rent, it may keep you focused on building a house. It's very easy to get fed up with the planning permission delays and put things on hold indefinitely.

Live in a mobile home on the farm

✔ Once initial outlay is paid, the costs are minimal and it will have a re-sale value too.

✔ It's going to be very convenient for calving/lambing if just beside the farmyard.

✘ Mobile homes can be freezing cold in winter so expect heating bills to be high.

✘ It's a very compact living space.

Move in with your parents

This might be to share the house with them temporarily while building is going on, or it could be long term.

✔ It saves money, which could keep you very happy.

✔ It makes sense if the house is a considerable size and you have only to build on a couple of rooms.

✔ Your parents will have company and the security of having you in the house.

✘ There will be a lack of privacy even if there are no communal areas.

✘ It could be difficult to enforce clear boundaries. Pigs might fly, in fact.

✘ Two women sharing a kitchen? Good luck! Okay, I'm probably being a little hasty and a little harsh. It will be fine while your other half is working and before you have children but sharing a kitchen is unlikely to work long term. Why? It would be rare (and very fortuitous) to find two women with the same standards of cleanliness and tidiness. What is just a bit of dust to one is filth to the other. One favours keeping the kitchen table clear; the other prefers to use the end of the kitchen table as a filing cabinet. One prefers to stack the mugs facing up; the other stacks them facing down. One will leave the kitchen spotless after an afternoon of baking; the other prefers to relax with a book, a cup of tea and a slice of cake for an hour before doing the washing-up. These are all small things but the small things mount up.

✘ It's probably not something you've given thought to, but two families (in reality, two women) sharing a washing line is not the stuff of harmony. They will hang clothes differently: one will hang trousers from the waistband and the other will hang them by the trouser legs. One will leave the pegs on the line and the other will put them in a bag and bring them into the house. The only time they should access the other person's clothes line is if it is going to lash rain and she knows the clothes are just dry. Ideally, neither one should be able to see the other's clothes from their side of the house, nor should they drive past it. Leaving out clothes for three days while they dry, get wet, dry and get wet again is extreme carelessness to one and just life to the other. If tension has built up between them, they will be fighting over washing line space on fine days. One will put on five loads of washing and be up at dawn hanging them out. Then the other will hang her clothes out at midnight. You might think there is a lot more to worry about in life than getting clothes dry, but trust me on this.

As you can tell, there's no easy solution to where you should live! Consider all options very carefully. Don't worry, there is lots more material to come on ensuring your wife and mother get on well.

Pigs might fly.

No chance of it happening. Often used sarcastically.

GIVE YOUR WEDDING A FARM THEME

The thorny question of the pre-nup is settled. The tricky question of where you are going to live is resolved. Now it's time to navigate through the wedding plans.

You're going to be living on the farm for evermore, do you really need a farm-themed wedding too? Of course you do! It's those little touches that add to the fun of the wedding and cement your relationship as Ideal Farm Husband and Perfect Farm Wife.

Transport

This can depend on the cleanliness and polish of the vehicle. I suggest rather than hiring a very posh limousine or a vintage car, scrub your tractor and drive her from the church to the reception in it. Just make sure you've informed the hotel so there's room to park it in the car park! Maybe don't spring it on your bride as a surprise in case she doesn't like the idea of getting on a tractor in a light-coloured wedding dress.

Another option would be just to have your photographs taken standing beside the tractor or another piece of machinery that will symbolise your life together.

Wedding colours

Most weddings seem to have the men's ties and buttonholes co-ordinating with the colour of the bridesmaid's dresses, but how about co-ordinating with your tractor? Green and yellow for a John Deere, for example?

Wedding cake

Most couples get the standard bride and groom cake toppers but you could get them with a farm theme. Choose from a ewe and ram or a cow and bull, or a bride and groom sitting on a tractor, accompanied by a trusty sheepdog.

You can add fun to the cake itself by decorating the sides with cows, sheep, goats and tractors.

Another idea is to display the cake on a tree trunk slice instead of a cake stand for some extra rustic charm and the perfect finishing touch. However, it's probably best to buy a purposely prepared and varnished one, not just one from the woodland on the farm. You don't want woodlice or ants suddenly appearing.

Wedding invitations and place cards

A picture of two farm animals – perhaps in pencil or charcoal – on the wedding invitation can be a nice touch. Or if your girlfriend comes from a dairy farm and you're a sheep farmer, then perhaps four animals: two cows and two sheep.

Think about shape as well as design: something as simple as paper shaped like a farm animal would be effective. Alternatively miniature animal (cows, sheep, goats, etc.) figures could each hold a place card and they could double as wedding favours too as each person brings home a farm animal toy as a memento.

Decorating the wedding venue

Adding a rustic touch to the decor of your wedding venue will emphasise the farming theme without going over the top. You could put flowers in miniature milk churns instead of vases. Large milk churns can be used to display bigger floral arrangements near the top table.

Old baler twine (not the bright blue type) wrapped around bottles for vases or a little bit of twine around the wedding bouquets and button holes would add a nice touch.

If you're getting married in the autumn, a harvest theme with sheaves of corn, pumpkins and autumn foliage would be very striking.

Wedding photographs

Every couple gets their photographs taken by a picturesque river or surrounded by beautiful blooms. You can do that too but with a farm theme. If you're lucky enough to have a field of golden corn or a field with rustic gates and old trees beside the venue, it will be ideal. If not, it's just a case of identifying suitable props near the wedding venue or bringing them along. They could include: a bale of straw or hay to sit on or stand beside, a new or vintage tractor, an old steam engine, a rustic gate or a wooden fence.

I heard of an American bride who brought her favourite cow along with a garland of flowers around her neck – while it sounds lovely, I can't see it being that easy to manage.

Photo booths with fun props are good fun at weddings and are becoming very popular. It's a lovely way for the guests to get photographs of themselves but also for the bride and groom to get copies too. By providing farming type clothes and props to match the farm theme, it will create lots of laughter.

LINES FOR YOUR WEDDING SPEECH

Wedding guests enjoy a good speech, particularly if they are relatively short and include a few jokes. They've had a lovely meal and a glass or two of wine. They are feeling mellow and ready to enjoy witty and fun speeches which also show how much the couple love each other and the high opinion their families and friends have of them.

Being so relaxed, they will laugh at almost any joke but if you want to bring the house down, add some farming one-liners and stories. It will make your speech memorable too. After all, if you are trying to attain the role of Ideal Farm Husband, you'd better demonstrate that your beloved is a Perfect Farm Wife.

Here are some to try for size:

- ○ I knew Melanie was a keeper: she was able to stand in a gap on our second date.

- ○ The day Sarah cooked me six potatoes, a rib roast and three vegetables I knew I couldn't let her go.

- ○ Wendy stood out a mile when I saw her at our local agricultural show and I couldn't take my eyes off her. Was it her dazzling smile, her brown eyes, her beautiful figure? Well, naturally I noticed them – who wouldn't? But it was her bright pink wellies that I thought would give our farmyard a blast of colour and pizzazz. As long as she came with them of course.

õ The fact Rachel can make a rhubarb tart/chocolate cake that's just as good as my mother's meant I knew she was the one for me.

õ Have you ever sorted cattle with someone for the first time? Or even with someone who is supposed to know the cattle well (indicate your father)? Managed to do it without arguing or shouting? Well, when Rachel was able to interpret my shouting "the black one" and she knew a little black and white heifer calf was the blackest of the three, I knew we'd make a great farming couple. Telepathy works!

õ I've been told a lot of things are cheaper than a divorce. Laura heard that too so guess what she bought me for a wedding gift? No, we didn't get a pre-nuptial agreement. She bought me a good working dog so it can do the running and listen to my shouts when things go wrong rounding up sheep/cattle.

õ Some people may think Linda is worth half a farm now but she's really much the poorer for marrying me; she now owns half the debt too!

õ Marriage is a celebration of love. It's also about being able to work together without killing each other when dosing calves, and being able to run faster than any of the runaway cattle. Laura's strength and speed means we're going to get along like a house on fire. Did you know she won the 1500m and the discus at school?

õ I first met Caitriona at our local agricultural show. How did I know she was the perfect woman for me? Was it her zebra striped wellies? Was it that streak of muck on her jeans that made me realise she would fit in perfectly on the farm? Was it the fact that she was leading a prize-winning Hereford heifer around the ring? Hmm, that one got my attention all right! However, it was her dazzling smile and her beautiful brown eyes that really swept me away.

○ Did you know that marrying a teacher in the 1970s was equivalent to getting an extra 20 cows that you didn't have to milk? Yes, her income equalled 20 cows. It must be equal to 200 now so that's my expansion sorted!

○ Have you ever heard this piece of advice? Never approach a bull from the front, a horse from behind or a fool from any direction? As Wendy is the perfect farm wife, I know now that I'm no fool.

○ I first met Susan at a fundraising event but romance didn't blossom that day. I wasn't exactly looking my best. A cow was calving and I was late. Instead of having a hot shower with sweet smelling shower gel, I discovered the water was cold and ended up having a quick wash. Susan revealed afterwards that the first thing she noticed about me was the lump of cow manure behind my ear and it didn't inspire her to stick around. Luckily, the water was hot the next time we met.

THE A–Z OF LIFE ON THE FARM

Congratulations: you have proposed and she has accepted. You're planning the wedding. She's visited the farm and has an idea of what life is going to be like. It's not as easy as just working out the guest list for your wedding or deciding where you're going to live.

If she comes from a farming background she may have an idea of what to expect and she might be telling you how her father did things, which could get a tad irritating after a while.

If she was brought up on a small dairy farm, she's going to find life on a large arable farm extremely different.

If she's not used to life on a farm, you may find there is some adjusting you both have to do. Here are some tips for helping her prepare and acclimatise and yes, you might have to make some changes too.

A A family affair

She's not just marrying you. She's marrying into the farm, which means the land, the animals, the crops and your family. As the bride moving into the family home, she's expected to honour the family name, produce the heir and the spare, look after her parents-in-law, keep her husband in the manner to which he was accustomed, bring in an income or work all hours on the farm, and be happy to see any siblings or other relatives that drop in or visit for extended holidays.

Don't tell her this before you get married in case she runs a mile but show your appreciation when she entertains all the prodigal sons and daughters. Recognise that you have it easy; you can clear out of the house making an excuse to milk the cows or harvest some corn.

B Bereavement

Unfortunately, tragic deaths occur in rural communities. People draw breath in shock and come together to support the bereaved family in whatever way they can, be it helping with funeral arrangements, taking care of work on the farm, preparing food for the wake and sharing in the grief. Rural funerals tend to be very large.

If it's an elderly person who died and the circumstances aren't tragic, country people enjoy a good funeral. They come together to give the deceased a good send off. First they visit the wake to sympathise with the family and sit at the dining room or kitchen table for a cup of tea, sandwiches and cake. Then they attend the funeral service and sometimes, depending on how well they know the family and how busy they are, they accept the invitation for refreshments back at the community hall, local pub or hotel. If your partner comes from a town or a different country, she might be surprised at the size of rural funerals.

One wonders how many generations it will take until the family are shaking their heads in sorrow at the lack of mourners and saying in surprise "but he had so many friends on Facebook".

C Colours

She chooses paint colours with poetic names like Light Chiffon, Green Melody and Skimming Stone, you prefer the simplicity of Massey Red, Deere Green or Holland Blue.

D Dogs

You think your dog has a great life: lots of exercise, plenty of rub downs when it has finished work and the best of meaty leftovers. She's shocked that the dinner bowl is an old biscuit tin, the dog never gets branded food, and the annual "grooming" is a hose down followed by a haircut with the shears used for the cows' tails. She's afraid to introduce you to her terrier in case you think it is going to earn its keep catching vermin up the yard.

E Exercise

While city slickers pass their lunchtimes or evenings pounding a treadmill at the gym, you don't need to, well, as long as you aren't sitting on a tractor or quad all day every day. A pedometer will let you know how you do in the walking stakes. Not only does farming save you time travelling to the gym and time spent there, you're saving on membership fees and you're exercising in the open air. She's a bit sceptical until you send her on a long walk to the far field to move a fence.

F Facts of life

Farm kids tend to discover the facts of life during the breeding season on the farm. Parents need to advise their sons that it's a bit more refined when it comes to a woman!

Farmers think they have a good understanding of what happens during a birth. However, don't ask the midwife if a "jack" or "chains" are used during childbirth. And no, do not expect a baby to come out hands first – have you seen how short a baby's arms are compared to their head size?

No matter how tired you are, don't even dream of nodding off for a nap during labour.

G The good life

Do farmers live an even larger version of "the Good Life"?[60] Do they escape from the pressures of the rat race? Is it a healthy lifestyle full of simple pleasures? Do they lead a sustainable lifestyle producing their own vegetables, fruits, meat and dairy products? Or is it a business like any other, capable of going under if it doesn't make enough of an income?

I think there's some truth in each of those questions. Farms have to make money to reinvest and improve, as well as provide a salary. But it has all the extra benefits of "the good life" if there is time for growing vegetables and producing pet lambs for meat.

How much of a Tom and Barbara are both of you? I have to admit I am a soft touch at times. Our three hens have provided us with eggs for the last two and a half years, even laying during the winter. They have a good life, locked in securely at night safe from predators, fed layers pellets, free to roam all day, protected from predators by our two dogs. One has stopped laying completely, one provides soft shelled eggs that they have got into the habit of eating and one lays one huge egg about once a week. If I were a "proper" or "traditional" farm wife, I'd have them cooking in the pot but instead I'm letting them enjoy a graceful retirement. Which would you expect her to do?

I guess even "commercial farmers" can let the principles of a "good life" support their decisions sometimes.

H Holidays

Did your parents and grandparents go on holiday? When we were children, it was rare for entire families to go on a holiday together. Sometimes the mother took the children to a relative for a few days or the children were sent to stay with cousins. There was no peer pressure among children or adults to get away on holiday. Now people see the benefits of getting away from it all and believe they work hard enough the rest of the year to deserve a week away.

Just because farmers in previous generations didn't go on holiday doesn't mean they would have said no to a break away though. In 1942, an irate farmer felt the three months holidays for teachers was two months too long while hard-working farmers didn't even get a day off. His solution: let them help with the ploughing, or eat less!

Sunday Independent 5 July 1942

If the farmers go on holiday for three months every year, who will feed all the teachers in their various schools and colleges? What do they give in return for all we give them? We rarely have a holiday in a lifetime. It is about time we woke up and made the others give a hand in the ploughing. If not, they must eat less.

If you think that one night away at Stony Sand Beach is a good holiday away from the farm, you're going to have to up your game. And just so you know – a holiday for your wife is not a two-night stay at the hospital having a baby, even if she has booked herself into a private room.

I Independence

You're your own boss; you don't have to answer to anyone. Or do you? The problem is, farmers are kind of screwed from all angles as we're price-takers most of the time. Meat, milk and grain prices are dictated by world supply and demand; however, the price we pay for purchases only goes up.

Your wife's friends and acquaintances might be PAYE workers: those who get a regular salary, a bonus at Christmas, paid holidays during the year, work nine to five for five days a week; and you're trying to explain why being your own boss is preferable for you. So what is it about farming, despite its lack of financial security, that makes it your choice over more lucrative regular work? It's a combination of these, perhaps:

- The peace and quiet.
- Working with nature and experiencing the change of the seasons.
- Being able to work in the open air.
- The short commute from farmhouse to farmyard.
- The fact no two days are ever the same.
- Meeting and overcoming challenges on a daily basis.

- The enjoyment of working together as a family.

- The interest in seeing your livestock improve with each generation.

- Seeing the circle of life every year with births of livestock each spring.

- Creating goals and reaching them.

- Being able to make your own decisions (well, as long as they adhere to the Department of Agriculture's rules).

- Knowing you are producing a good-quality food product for others to enjoy.

- Working with large machinery.

- Being your own boss.

J Joking

Farming is hard work and involves long hours for much of the year. Sometimes you need to have some fun to prevent it feeling like drudgery. They say laughter is the best medicine and it can really make you feel good. After all, if you can find the fun, the job becomes a game doesn't it? Playing jokes on each other doesn't take up much time either.

Our son Will loves acting the maggot with his dad. He sneaks up behind Brian and shouts a loud "boo" in his ear. The higher Brian jumps, the louder Will laughs. One day, Brian decided to get his own back. Dusk was coming on and he hid behind the sliding door in the meal shed. As Will strolled in, swinging his two buckets, I heard a loud "boo" and a shriek followed by an irritated yell and raucous guffaws.

Water fights are good fun too, especially if one has a hose and the other a number of buckets of water! Wouldn't that be frowned upon in an office?

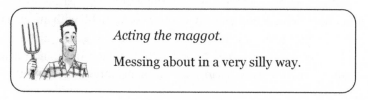

Acting the maggot.

Messing about in a very silly way.

K Kitchen

The farm kitchen is the hub of the home, a multi-purpose room where family and friends gather. It's for cooking and eating, where homework is done and where friends join you for a scone and a cup of tea. The armchair by the wood burning stove is the perfect place for a tired farmer to rest for a few minutes after his dinner.

However, it's often an unofficial office too and this is where opinions can differ between husband and wife. Some people like to clear off a kitchen table after a meal and leave it completely bare. All paperwork is relegated to the official office.

And then there are some people (like me) who prefer to collapse with a cup of tea and a slice of warm rhubarb tart as they ignore the teetering piles of unopened bills, letters, newspapers, half-read book, replacement calf tags, the latest "handmade gift" from a child in school, the little white book, half a packet of biscuits, three pens that don't work and a jar of jam, all at the end of the table.

It is very important that you decide on this together when you are "courting". Are you a "completely clear table" couple or are you a "let it build up, clear and let it build up again" couple? Unless you are off the same ilk, there will be casualties.

Oh, and while we're on this topic, she may believe that all farmhouse kitchens must have an Aga.

L Lie-on

It's not very often a farmer gets a lie-on but if he tries, something is bound to disturb it. Once, having been up until 3am after a long day at silage, Brian decided life was too short to get up at 6am and set the alarm for 7:45.

We woke at the sound of a jeep in the yard. A gate had been left open from a silage field to the road. The cattle in the adjoining field, having decided the yellow field with luscious green hedges needed investigating when all had gone quiet, had broken through the fence, found the open gate and gone for a stroll up to the main road. Luckily a neighbour had spotted them, herded them into his own field and come up to let us know. Of course, it had to have been the neighbour who never has a lie-on, no matter how late the bedtime hour!

The fact that 7:30 is a lie-on may take your new wife a while to get used to.

M Meal times

Meals vary in both name and time between town and country.

Those working 9–5 tend to have:

🍁 Breakfast before they leave for work.

🍁 Sandwich or salad lunch at 1pm.

🍁 Dinner in the evening.

🍁 Maybe a cup of tea or a glass of wine around 9:30.

Those living on farms do it rather differently:

🍁 Breakfast (sometime between 6am and 8am).

🍁 Elevenses or second breakfast (sometime between 9:30 and 11am) – tea, toast, brown bread and scones.

🍁 Dinner (1pm) – meat, potatoes and two vegetables followed by a home-made dessert, tea and cake (or biscuits).

🍁 Afternoon tea (4pm) – tea, brown bread and jam, followed by cake or scones. (In some households, a bell was used to signal that afternoon tea was ready.)

🍁 Tea (usually round about 7pm, or at 5pm if no afternoon tea) – this is a meal, not just a cup of tea. It is usually something like the following: a "grill" which is rasher, sausage and fried egg; beans on toast; scrambled or poached egg on toast; two boiled eggs; a salad; or cheese and crackers. There will be at least two types of bread (home-made soda bread and a shop-bought sliced pan) served with real butter, home-made jam and mugs of tea, finishing off with scones, Victoria sponge or apple tart.

🍁 Supper (around 10pm) – this will be whatever is in the fridge. It might be a left-over-roast-beef sandwich, cheese and crackers, or a slice of cake and a large cup of tea.

Imagine how she might feel coming from a three-meal a day household with perhaps just a cup of tea or glass of wine late in the evening to trying to circumnavigate your meal times in a household where there's two breakfasts, elevenses, dinner, a cup of tea at 4, tea at 7ish and a light supper before bed!

It doesn't mean she can't change it. I've succeeded in getting it down to three meals and an occasional snack. Our favourite meal is breakfast at around 10am. We feel we've achieved a reasonable amount of work so can enjoy a good breakfast and use the time to plan the work for the rest of the day, chat about the kids, groan about the number of bills just arrived in the post (or possibly all three). It's almost always a leisurely and chatty meal as we put the world to rights.

N **Neighbourhood watch**
In towns, neighbourhood watch meant communities looked out for suspicious characters and risk of theft. Rural neighbourhood watch was when you got a call to say your sheep had escaped from their field and were out on the road. Unfortunately, its meaning has now changed in rural areas as farms are hit with thefts of machinery, tools, cattle and diesel. Rural neighbours still keep an eye out for each other though. We were rounding up cattle recently to bring them in for TB testing and a neighbour rang to check if everything was all right as he heard the noise and wondered if a wild dog was after the calves. The consideration was appreciated as you just never know what could be happening.

Neighbourhood watch also involves your every move being monitored, in a "goldfish bowl" kind of way, something that may take your spouse some time to get used to. If she's moving into the area, the neighbourhood watch will be extra vigilant (i.e. nosy).

O **Orienteering**
You call it bringing you a spare tractor part or a meal when you're working in one of the fields. She calls it an orienteering exercise as she tries to work out how to get from

the "Quarry Field" to the "Round Field" and through that to the "Field at the Back". If, like me, she's the type to get lost going from a city hotel to the car park one street away where the car was parked two days previously, she might find it a challenge. It's not like your fields are marked on Google Maps. In an ideal world, a perfect farm wife possesses excellent map-reading skills and, of course, you need to give her a folio map of the farm with all the field names written in.

P Pocket money

Pocket money, that monetary bribe to get kids to do some jobs, take some responsibility and discover how little they can buy with a couple of quid. Your non-farming other half probably got pocket money for tasks such as keeping her room tidy, hoovering the house, washing the car, cleaning windows and emptying the dishwasher. Maybe she cut grass and weeded flower beds too.

You earned your pocket money for full days of work. You did all of the above as well as the following: stacked the square hay and straw bales, covered silage pits, dosed cattle, sheared sheep, herded all the livestock, power washed sheds, helped to bring stock to the mart, milked cows and cleaned out the henhouse. Graduating to being able to drive the tractor meant at last you could sit down on the job. At least you were hardly ever in your bedroom to make it untidy!

Q Quarrels

Arguments and quarrels are fairly inevitable when you're working together on a farm. I like to describe it as "bickering and getting annoyance out of your system". Things go wrong and someone gets the blame. In frustration, the angry person often puts too much blame on the poor person who made the mistake. If she hates arguments or grew up in a household where trading insults was rare, it's going to be very hard for her to get used to it. She might even believe it's her fault that she can't understand your hand gestures from the tractor or recognise which ewe is the biggest. It's important the person at the receiving end of it is capable of retaliating, of standing her ground or of turning and walking away and leaving you in the middle of the cattle and sheep to fend for yourself.

On the first day of letting cows out to grass this spring, Brian was off putting up a temporary fence and I was feeding calves. I came out of the calf shed to see about 40 cows galloping down the avenue having pushed open the sliding door. I raced after them but luckily my mother had spotted them and run out to stop them at the road gate. So far so good. Having turned the cows around, I followed them back up the avenue. But I'd forgotten the open garden gate and yes, 40 cows (160 hooves) were delighted at this unexpected excursion and hurtled round and round the garden.

Brian was incensed I had been so daft to not realise they'd go into the garden. The more he ranted and raved, the more I laughed till I was doubled. Yes, I had been silly and yes, it was so typical that curious cows would decide to investigate. But there was no point in Brian being cross, the damage was done.

We put a mini roller behind the lawnmower and gave the lawn a run over with that. Even so, while strolling around the garden recently, I twisted an ankle by walking into one of the holes! My comeuppance perhaps. I'm sure Brian thought so, though he had the good sense not to say it.

There are times when both of you have to bite your tongue. For example, there's no point in having an argument when doing the milking and milk recording together as it will only distress and agitate the cows and you'll end up being sprayed with all kinds of excrement. Always pick your moment (and I don't mean when your beloved is behind a cow).

R Retail therapy

Whether a person's idea of retail therapy is perusing all the machinery at a large agricultural show, or spending the day at a shopping centre, you might find that as a couple your ideas don't coincide – sometimes you just have to give each other the opportunity to do your own thing.

S Safety

She learnt how to cross the road, travel on public transport and never to talk to strangers. You also learnt not to go near the field with the bull in it, how to wriggle under or jump over barbed wire, how to test whether or not an electric wire was on, and to stay out of the farmyard unless an adult knew you were there. Dangers included being chased by a cockerel or a gander, realising you were in a field with the bull, getting your boots stuck in mud, falling into nettles, tearing your jeans on barbed wire, getting clothes snagged by blackberry brambles, falling off a trailer, being kicked by a cow, being head butted by a sheep and bitten by a goat.

I'm sure our workman Tommy thought the trailer was securely attached to the tractor when he lifted me onto the trailer when I was six. I was as happy as a pig in muck as we rattled our way down the avenue and on to a narrow road on our way to the out-farm. And then we were attached no more and the trailer shuddered its way down the hill to stop on a stone bridge with the river looking very near. Whether he heard me or just sensed a weight was missing from the tractor, I'm not sure, but Tommy looked back and did a double take to see the trailer about a hundred feet behind him. Never one to fuss, he calmly reversed the tractor, found the pin on the ground further up the road, rested the drawbar on a big stone and lifted it up to the right height to push the pin home again.

All farmers of my generation will have stories from their childhood of near accidents. Unfortunately, there will be some stories where the accident wasn't a near one but a serious one. There seem to be more tragic deaths within farming now and we need to be mindful that the dangers are very real. More haste means more chance of dying today. A sobering thought.

Happy as a pig in muck.

When someone is doing their favourite job or pastime, even if it involves some mess. Very happy.

T Time

There's a world of difference between town time and farm time. Have you ever noticed townspeople tend to arrive for appointments or visits on time? This habit probably started many decades ago when adherence to the clock became more important with the introduction of train timetables. Bristol was 11 minutes behind London until there were trains running between the two places. Dublin time was 25 minutes behind London time until The Time (Ireland) Act was passed in 1916. Farmers were just one group who weren't happy about losing 25 minutes to the English!

Trains left according to a timetable, shops opened and closed at specific times and exact timings were important for telegraphy. Therefore, townspeople formed the habit of punctuality more effectively than rural dwellers. Rural shops might open on time but it's doubtful they close at the time it says on the door. You grew up knowing "I'll just be five minutes" meant at least 30 and that it was almost deemed rude to arrive at someone else's house on time. What if they were running late? In any case, something always went wrong just as you were about to leave the house – a sheep might be sick, some cattle got out or a cow decided to start calving.

You'll probably find you have a much more relaxed attitude to time than your girlfriend has. I hope she has better levels of patience than you do.

U Umbrella holding

She sees it as normal to carry a small umbrella in a handbag; you wonder if it could be used as a stick when she is standing in the gap.

V Vehicle

As a couple, you'll probably have two vehicles, one being her car and the other being your farm car/jeep/truck. Hers is immaculate. Yours might save lives during an apocalypse: there are tools and baler twine to build makeshift shelters, old farming leaflets to start a fire, dregs of medicine in old bottles to tend the sick, and squashed and forgotten-about food lurking somewhere – the crumbs alone could sustain life. Her car might turn heads but would be useless in an emergency.

W Weather forecast

As a child, bad weather probably only bothered her if they couldn't play outside, but for you it meant the difference between good humours and a successful harvest or short tempers, less money, more stress and a lot of extra work. The weather forecast slot after the news was treated with reverence in your house. Everyone knew to listen in complete silence. You were all aware it would influence the work for the next few days if not longer. Tapping the barometer to see if it was on its way up was a habit the whole family had.

We can now check weather forecasts using multiple methods, just to see if they are all the same! Unfortunately, the weather forecasters never seem to know what will happen and use phrases like "occasional scattered showers" and "sunny spells" to ensure they cover all eventualities.

Your wife might be bemused by this obsession with the weather for a time, but she will soon become as transfixed with the forecasts as you are.

X Xmas

Christmas mornings are usually very different in farm households (unless you are tillage farmers) to non-farming ones. She probably opened all her presents first thing on Christmas morning as her family gathered in the living room. They then played with their gifts to their hearts' content, only interrupted by a request to get dressed and go to Mass or to eat their dinner.

You opened your gifts from Santa first but you weren't allowed to open any others until all the farm work was done. You may even have had to wait until dinner was eaten and the washing-up done so that everyone's work was finished and the whole family could enjoy the gift-opening together.

It might be wise to talk about this before your first Christmas together, especially if she is a lover of the festive season.

Y Yoke

In Ireland, a yoke is anything that you need right now and you can't think of its name. "Pass me that yoke, would you. No, that thing, that yoke, right there." It will take her time to work out what a yoke is, never mind which particular yoke you might be referring to at that moment. Patience is required. Better still, know the names of everything you might need.

Z ZZZZZ

You can generally survive on much less sleep than a non-farmer. You know the value in a 15-minute power nap after a meal that will keep you going for another eight hours. You realise sleep will be in short supply at various times of the year and your body adjusts to cope. You know this stage of the year will pass and life will return to normal. Your girlfriend may be wondering if life will ever be the same again as yet another date is cancelled or you fall asleep on her shoulder in the cinema.

You need sleep to function and to be safe but if you know she's really going to get annoyed because you're sleeping the only time she sees you, you've got to either build more time for her into your day or take some time off before the busy season and warn her what's coming. Farm wives can feel like widows during busy seasons!

If you get really tired when driving, it's much safer to stop and take a nap especially if you know you're running on empty. On a hot summer's day many years ago, my dad decided to take a 15-minute nap lying on the grass beside the tractor. He was snoozing peacefully until he was awoken by a panicked shout. A visiting cousin, out for a ramble, had spotted him lying down and thought he'd had a heart attack. Maybe you should stay in the tractor to have your power nap!

QUIZ (FOR HIM)

1. It's cold out and she looks like a Michelin Man as she's wearing so many layers. She also has muck splattered across her face. Do you:
    (a) Tell her you love her and she's never looked more beautiful? ❑
    (b) Burst out laughing and pass her a roll of blue paper to wipe her face? ❑
    (c) Suggest she looks in the mirror? ❑

2. She makes a mistake in the paperwork when registering a calf, putting it down as male instead of female. Do you:
    (a) Say: "Mistakes like that happen all the time, it isn't the first time and it won't be the last."? ❑
    (b) Comment: "Someone in the department will have a bit of a conniption about that."? ❑
    (c) Ask: "Since when did an F look like an M?" ❑

3. She's milking with you for the first time. Do you:
    (a) Give her the quietest ones to milk? ❑
    (b) Tell her which ones kick out? ❑
    (c) Let her find out herself which cows cough and send excrement flying across the parlour with remarkable aim? ❑

4.   It's a bad year for milk/meat/grain prices. Do you:
   (a)   Shrug and say: "At least there won't be as much going to the tax man."?   ❑
   (b)   Cut spending to a minimum and make an appointment to see the bank manager?   ❑
   (c)   Ask her if she can get more overtime and put the house building plans on hold, saying you can both live with your mother for another year?   ❑

5.   You're planning to give your fiancée a gift to welcome her to the farm: Will it be:
   (a)   A pair of flowery wellies (with something nice inside like perfume or jewellery)?   ❑
   (b)   A heifer calf of her own?   ❑
   (c)   A pair of plain blue wellies and her very own pitchfork?   ❑

6.   The wedding is coming up and your part in the organising is:
   (a)   To say yes to everything she requests: farm cake topper, milk churns, sunflowers, a pet sheep as a ring bearer ...   ❑
   (b)   To clean the tractor, arrange for it to be brought to the church and drive it to the reception; oh, and find milk churns for the flower arrangements.   ❑
   (c)   Your mother is doing your side of it.   ❑

How did you do?

Mostly A's – You've lots of patience for helping her adjust to farming life and become a perfect farm wife.

Mostly B's – You have great intentions but may need to put in more effort with some of your gestures.

Mostly C's – You need to read this book again, paying more attention. Repeat after me: "Make her feel special, make her feel special, make her feel special."

QUIZ (FOR HER)

1. He asks you to bring him a dinner to the field. You pack a picnic and it consists of:
    (a) Crackers and cheese, grapes, prosecco, and a chocolate mousse with strawberries for dessert. ❑
    (b) Doorstep sandwiches and a flask of tea. ❑
    (c) A beef casserole with jacket potatoes followed by half a sponge cake and a flask of tea. ❑

2. Your fiancé gave you two pet lambs this year. You have named them:
    (a) Romeo and Cupid. ❑
    (b) Tom and Jerry. ❑
    (c) Chops and Gravy. ❑

3. Your wedding day "something old, something new, something borrowed and something blue" would be:
    (a) An old coin, the wedding dress, a bracelet from your mum and a blue garter. ❑
    (b) Your antique engagement ring, the wedding dress, the veil and light blue, hand-painted shoes. ❑
    (c) The vintage tractor, diamond earrings, the wedding dress and blue baler twine (tied around the milk churn). ❑

4. He asks you to put some oil on the wrapped bales in the field to keep the crows away while he goes to get the bale loader. Do you:

   (a) Get your hand-pressed virgin olive oil with herbs and put two dots of it on each bale? ❏

   (b) Get some vegetable oil and pour it liberally over each bale? ❏

   (c) Get some old waste oil from the yard, pour it into a bottle, puncture a hole in the lid and give each bale a couple of good squirts? ❏

5. A mouse jumps out from behind the bales and corners you. What do you do?

   (a) Scream like a hyena and run. ❏

   (b) Take deep breaths and sidle away making a mental note to stay clear of that corner in future. ❏

   (c) Ignore it – it's only a mouse. ❏

6. You decide that to be a true farmer's wife, you must have hens, hence you commandeer him to build you a hen coop and arrive with:

   (a) Three hens and a cockerel as you believe a cockerel is needed for the hens to produce eggs. ❏

   (b) A dozen hens in various breeds. ❏

   (c) Four Rhode Island Red hens and a bag of layers pellets. ❏

How did you do?

Mostly A's – You're wonderful for trying so hard. You just need to read *How To Be A Perfect Farm Wife* and you'll get there.

Mostly B's – You have great intentions and try your best.

Mostly C's – As perfect as Mary Poppins, should she have decided to become a farm wife.

PART SIX

BEING AN IDEAL FARM HUSBAND

HOW TO STAY MARRIED

Huge congratulations: you're home from the honeymoon and looking forward to starting married life together!

Listen up for a second though. I'm sure plenty of people have told you that no matter how much you love someone, it takes a bit of adjustment to get used to living with them. Imagine, then, the adjustments your wife has to make: not only has she married you, but she has also married your farm, the dog, your livestock, your crops and your family. The pre-marriage course may not have prepared her for all that!

This section is all about helping you attain Ideal Farm Husband status, at least in the eyes of your wife, and preparing you for a long and happy married life together.

Yes, I know it's not one-sided, it's not all down to you, but hopefully your spouse will already have read *How To Be A Perfect Farm Wife* and will have a head start.

HOW TO BE ROMANTIC

Farmers are probably better known for being gruff than being romantic; if you fall into that category I'm going to show you how to change all that. The trick to being romantic as a farmer is to do little things that are considerate and show your wife you are thinking of her. It's not necessarily about big gestures like buying bouquets of roses or whisking her off to exotic locations on a regular basis (although it's doubtful she would refuse either one).

Here's how you can show her you are thinking of her:

- Consider what she might need when you are in the farm store, perhaps new boots or strawberry plants for the garden. Saying "I saw these and thought you would like them" is going to make her feel special and loved. It works both ways of course; she might do the same for you when she's shopping.

- Bring her wildflowers from the hedges or cottage flowers from the garden.

- Bring in the clothes from the washing line if it looks like it's going to rain. Just make sure they don't hit off your dirty boots on the way in. Clean hands are a good idea too.

- Sit through her favourite TV show pretending to be interested. (Don't think that she doesn't do that for you.)

- Suggest going to the cinema when a film you know she wants to see is showing.

- When you're picking up parts for the tractor or visiting the mart, pop into a shop and spend a tenner on a bunch of flowers. It won't take long and it will make her feel special.

- Don't begrudge her a lie-on just because you have to get up at 6am. Leave the curtains drawn and tiptoe out. She will repay you later by letting you have a well-earned snooze while she's chauffeuring you somewhere.

- Light the fire half an hour before she's due home – little beats coming in to a welcoming fire and cosy living room.

- Some women need chocolate like they need oxygen. (I am one of these women.) Always have her favourite bar of chocolate (or other treat) hidden away somewhere for emergencies. Emergencies like when she's in a bad mood or a tad stressed. If you are able to miraculously produce her favourite comfort food in her time of need, you will be viewed as a man in a million. Now, that's romance!

- Some women prefer a new trailer or a pedigree heifer calf to jewellery, so ensure you know which type of woman she is. The advantage of the former gifts, of course, is they are tax deductible so you can spend even more on them.

- Use pink wrap for your silage bales.[61] It raises money for the Irish Cancer Society and many women see it as a romantic gesture.

- If she brings you a meal when you are working in the field, turn it into a romantic picnic by taking an extra ten minutes to chat and catch up on the news of the day.

- Spend time together on the farm every day. Moving temporary fences and bringing in the cows together is a nice way to fit a romantic walk into your day. It's all too easy to do these jobs separately as time is of the essence, but sometimes it's worth doubling up on the job so that you spend time together.

HOW TO ENJOY
MAINTENANCE DAYS

You both lead busy and hectic lives and there are times when you need to take time to recharge the batteries. It's good if you can take time off together and enjoy each other's company but there are times when time off should be very separate. While some men would be quite happy to visit a spa with their other half, wandering around in a white dressing gown and having a hot stone massage followed by a facial, it possibly isn't your cup of tea.

If a spa day is your wife's idea of heaven, then don't dismiss it as being a waste of time or money. She needs time to unwind and she'll come home rejuvenated and full of the joys of spring. But what about you? What can you do that will revitalise you in mind, body and spirit? You know that spending a day of uninterrupted maintenance on a tractor, tinkering around without anyone interrupting or shouting that dinner is ready is just what you need. So choose a Saturday (so you know there's no danger of salespeople calling) and book both of you in for separate, yet essential, maintenance days.

HOW TO ROMANCE ON THE MOST ROMANTIC DAY OF THE YEAR

What should you do on Valentine's Day? It falls smack in the middle of your busiest lambing and calving week when getting sleep is a priority, or you're working long days readying fields for sowing. While other couples are eating overpriced meals in crowded restaurants and/or give bouquets of flowers and big boxes of chocolates tied with elaborate bows, you are donning the lubricated rubber gloves. How, then, can you show her that you're capable of being romantic and making her feel special?

Be organised. If you'd like to send her flowers, order them in January. Buy the chocolates and hide them well! If you can't get away from the maternity unit, set up a couple of hay bales to sit on, a rug to keep you warm, a bottle of wine, two glasses and a picnic basket. Oh, and a flask of tea and two mugs. Don't forget the calving camera might be on a TV in your parents' house though, so don't get too frisky!

Our electricity went late one night last February just as the last cow had been milked and the calves had been fed. However, we still had to move the very "heavily pregnant and just about to pop" cows from the wintering shed to the calving unit. Determining which ones had to be moved, separating them and moving them across, all by torchlight and without spooking them, was a tricky job for two. On the plus side, we were spending some time together in a "dimly lit" setting!

HOW TO MINIMISE ARGUMENTS

One way to lessen the chance of arguments is to work out the things you shouldn't do. By avoiding these, you're also working on being romantic – kinda.

I heard recently of a divorced couple whose troubles could be traced back to him leaving a water glass on the worktop every time he had a drink. A minor infringement, you might think. Well, she had requested he rinse the glass and put it away in the cupboard each time. He felt there was no harm leaving it out but he failed to notice that to her it was an annoyance – one that grew a tiny bit each time he did it until it was once too often and she asked him for a divorce!

If a water glass can cause that much angst, imagine what your dirty wellies strewn across the back hall or your smelly, wet coat left to dry on the kitchen chair might start!

There are lots of things to argue about on a farm. If a squabble involves animals or the inability to give or understand directions, that's okay. Spats like that usually blow over in five minutes and help get irritation out of your systems.

Can some arguments be prevented? Yes! If you know what causes arguments, you can work at preventing them.

Causes of arguments

Stress

Stress is inevitable in farming. You think you have your day's work planned and either someone leaves a gate open and animals get out or one is sick, and before you know it you feel you've wasted about three hours. Except you haven't wasted it, you had to deal with those issues in the here and now.

There's so much we have no control over – world trade prices, the outcome of Brexit, the weather, the income tax rate. We can only deal with the controllables, such as: there being enough fodder saved for the winter, there being sufficient slurry storage, doing your best to optimise grass or crop growth, minimising spend but not to the level that it affects next year's profits, animal health and, indeed, your own health.

Are we our own worst enemies at times? Many farmers know they are not invincible but feel like they are supposed to be the stalwart person in the community, the one others look up to, the breadwinner in the family. We inherit a farm and give ourselves the task of improving it significantly before we hand it on to the next generation. We worry about what others think, and if things start to go awry the fear of failure and shame can take over. The farm can become a heavy millstone around the neck very quickly.

Stress itself is caused by all kinds of factors but your arguments might be caused by regular bursts of worry and tension. Do any of these sound familiar?

- The Post Factory Post Mortem – When the cheque comes back for the sheep or cattle and you wish you'd sold some a fortnight earlier or waited for another fortnight with others. What is done, is done. Learn from it if there's something to learn, or accept there will always be a couple that didn't kill out as you expected. Move on to the next one because yes, there's another stress around the corner.

◢ Pre Scanning Shakes – You're both going to feel a little nervous over the scanning, since it signals how the next year's finances will work out as you discover how many lambs/calves/goats will be born.

◢ Pre Silage Tension/Pre Harvest Tension/Pre Hay Making Stress – What will the weather do? Should you cut today or wait a couple of days? Not even the weather forecasters can tell you where exactly those scattered showers will fall, so it's a case of relying on Lady Luck sometimes too.

◢ Irritable Bank Manager Syndrome – Yes, it's annual review time, and even though you know the accounts inside out you're not looking forward to having to regurgitate it all when it's been a bad year. Our bank manager ushered us into his office once and said jokingly, "Come in to my parlour" and before I could stop myself, I replied "Said the spider to the fly". It can feel a bit like that sometimes.

◢ Pre Audit Ants in your Pants – Whether it's an audit for your finances or your farming paperwork, it's nerve-racking wondering if there's something you have overlooked. It can feel a little like going to the head teacher's office sometimes.

Because many of these happen monthly or annually, there's no wonder you might be seen as a bit of a drama queen for indulging in the same stresses year after year. The one good thing about farming is that you're usually so physically tired at the end of the day very little can keep you from sleeping.

I find the only way to deal with stresses like these is to do what you can to the best of your ability and then say "to hell with it". Once the cattle are sold or the silage is made, you just get on with the next stage of the farming year.

Childcare

We all know there is stress as well as joy in childrearing. It helps if you take an active part in it though. Your wife might tell you weeks in advance that you have to collect your daughter from school to bring her to the dentist or you need to bring your son to a party. The problem is, if she tells you too far in advance (this could be anything between three days to three weeks), you might forget. When she reminds you the night before and you delay removing that panic-stricken expression from your face by a millisecond, you're busted. Get into the habit of using an app on your phone to set up reminders!

Think of this scenario (or a variation of it) for a Saturday morning. She fed the calves while he milked and then she got the kids their breakfast. Lack of time meant she had to choose between clearing the table or taking a shower. While the kids were at football, she did the grocery shopping. He texted her with a request to collect supplies at the vet store, which she did before collecting the kids and heading home. She had to clear away the table and the worktop before she could even start to put the groceries away or begin cooking lunch. Then he walked in and casually asked was dinner ready yet, when all she wanted to do was collapse with a large cup of tea and a slice of cake. Does that ring a bell?

Women need cake (or maybe crisps or even chocolate), never forget that. Although offering her cake every evening because you're late in to help with the kids is not going to get you off the hook. And if she puts on weight, it will be your fault!

What can you do if she's working fewer hours than you, bringing home the bacon and doing nearly all the childcare (as is likely in a farming family)? When the farm work isn't so busy, be in early two evenings a week so you supervise the baths and do story time, and do one Saturday of activities a month. The kids (and you) will love it. Alternatively, plan your day so you can spend time with the children after school or at bedtime and then go back out to work.

Bringing home the bacon.

Earning a living and putting food on the table.

Tiredness

We all get narky when we're tired and there will be times of the year when you're running on empty in terms of energy levels. Go on a holiday or even a two-night break away before the busiest time of year so you recharge the batteries. Being able to take power naps is a useful skill.

Failed telepathy

Telepathy is great but only when it works perfectly. Don't rely on it all the time. Check you are on the same wavelength. Sometimes, just sometimes, your instructions are as clear as mud. Better to suffer her slight irritation because she thinks you're being ridiculously pedantic than having a shouted argument because sheep get out.

There was the evening I walked to the furthest field to open the gate for the cows but no cows arrived. I phoned Brian wondering why he hadn't let them on. Apparently I was supposed to remember a particular gate was open and I should have closed it. The cows had returned to the field they'd grazed that day – at the other end of the farm. The dog earned a good supper as he rounded up the cows for me!

While an ideal farm husband should comprehend every word his wife says or doesn't say, he must also communicate clearly so his wife can understand every word and every gesture perfectly.

Being late - again

Yes, this old chestnut. Late for meals, late in the evenings, late when you're both going out, arriving after the bride at a wedding. She's convinced you will be late for your own funeral.

You can't blame her really. You ask her to have dinner at 1:45 promptly as you've planned your day perfectly. Then you text her at 1:40 to say you'll be another hour and she's just about to serve up. Don't tell me it's never happened.

The best policy is to keep her informed – phone signal permitting. Things take longer than you think they will or something goes wrong such as having to treat a lame calf so the 20-minute job of herding turns into 45. Send a text to let her know and never, ever complain if dinner turns out to be burnt/dried up/fit only for the dog by the time you get in.

Some farm wives will serve dinner at a precise time each day and to be an Ideal Farm Husband you must arrive promptly. However, if that causes stress when something goes wrong and you know you're going to be late and she'll be fuming, you need to have a chat. It's nice to eat together, but it's not the end of the world if your dinner has to be reheated (unless it's pasta).

If she's left the kitchen tidy and gone to town, put your dirty dishes in the dishwasher before you go out again.

Oh, and a tip for the farm wife: if you want your husband to pop in, just sit down for ten minutes with a cup of tea and he's bound to arrive in asking what you've been doing all day.

Housework

Have you been mollycoddled? Can you boil an egg, iron a shirt, polish your shoes, cook a simple meal, wash the dishes, stack the dishwasher, find the washing powder, hoover the carpet, put a duvet cover on a double duvet and wash the kitchen floor? If you're answering no to some of these, you have been mollycoddled and no mistake.

These are the kind of things you need to be doing so you can pull your weight and be the envy of less fortunate wives:

- Don't leave dirty socks on the floor or under the bed.
- Put your dirty farm clothes in the "farm laundry" basket.
- Wash your farm clothes. (Those tongs in the corner? They are so your wife doesn't have to touch your working clothes.) You don't have to wash them in a river with carbolic soap – it's simple: learn how to use the washing machine.

⊿ Hang washing on the line occasionally.

⊿ Polish your own shoes.

⊿ Empty the dishwasher (only stack it if she isn't fussy, life is too short to be chastised for not stacking a dishwasher in a particular way).

⊿ Wash the kitchen floor, remembering to sweep it first. A steam cleaner is a great invention by the way, especially if your previous efforts with a mop required Noah's ark by the time you were finished.

⊿ Set and light the fire.

⊿ Put out the bins. I'm not sure why, but town husbands always get this job – must be a "manly job".

⊿ Wash the windows on the outside. (Wouldn't it be romantic if you wash the outside while she's washing the inside?)

⊿ Cook a simple tea like poached eggs on toast, baked potatoes or even just beans on toast.

Already doing your share of the housework? Great – you're pretty ideal as a husband. But if you don't know how to do some jobs on that list above, ask your wife to show you. Don't ask your mum as she will feel either a failure for not having taught you, or indignant that you aren't being looked after in the way to which you were accustomed. If you just pretend you know what you're doing, your wife may end up with pink or grey smalls, food poisoning and a flooded kitchen.

By the way, if you happen to marry a woman who is all too happy to do all the housework, hold on to her tight because they don't make them like that very often. Brian knows.

These are serious "string you up" offences:

⊿ She has vacuumed the house; you remember that you left something in a jeans pocket upstairs and run up to get it, leaving a trail of corn all the way up the stairs. Ask someone else to get it or strip off at the back door first!

◢ She has washed the kitchen floor, you "just nip in" to get something out of the fridge and don't bother to take off your mucky boots, tiptoeing across the floor thinking it won't be noticed. How could it not be noticed? Take off those boots!

◢ She hangs out two loads of washing before going to work or town and comes home to find that you've agitated slurry and the beautifully dry laundry reeks of it and needs to be washed again – a couple of times. Tell her if you're going to be working at slurry or dung.

◢ She has a list of things you said you'd help with in the quieter month or two on the farm. If that list stays the same year in, year out, with a few things added to the bottom each time, you are going to come to blows. So work your way through it in your next quiet period or else pay someone to do the jobs.

We have ten small panes of coloured glass either side of our hall door and three years ago, one was broken by a football hitting it. I had planned on changing them to a clear glass in any case, but repaired it with cardboard temporarily. Admittedly it took me ten months to get the glass for all 20 panes but Brian promised to replace them during his "quiet time". The broken one was replaced two years ago, the rest are still in a stack. I think I need to start taking pot shots at the other panes myself!

By the way, as the kids get older, giving control of the TV remote to whoever is doing the ironing is an effective way to get that job done, especially by sports-loving boys when a match is on! It works in this house!

Chauffeuring

She might get a bit irritated if she feels like your unpaid chauffeur, especially if you're either snoring your head off or giving a running commentary on everything that's over the hedges from your position in the passenger seat.

You need to make it up to her by giving her a lie-on occasionally or an uninterrupted nap (you entertain the kids). Then she will have the energy to stay awake while driving and you can catch up on your sleep (and your agricultural observations).

Ending up in a farmer's yard or the mart when she gives you control of the steering wheel while she has a nap isn't going to go down well either!

Not being rational

Don't take your anger for someone or something else out on your wife. It happens all too often that someone else irks you – your dad possibly, saying you sold cows too cheaply or bought sheep that were too expensive or you didn't plough a field properly. (Yes, it's all too easy to be an expert when you're watching someone else do something!) If you can't tell your dad where to go with his opinion, then go to a field and stomp around before you take it out on anyone else.

The advantage of farming is there are always a few cows or sheep in a distant field you can yell at (don't yell in the milking parlour or it'll make matters worse) and the walk and fresh air will help your mood! Kicking at a tractor tyre won't damage anything worse than your toe.

Feeling unappreciated

If we feel underappreciated, be it for the hours we work, the meals we prepare or our efforts in finishing something, it can make us very narky. If Brian says something like "that dinner didn't have much love in it" and I know I've thrown it together, it's not going to bother me (and I know he'll appreciate the next nice dinner all the more) but if I'd put a lot of effort into it, he's going to get a snarl in response.

Many women these days aren't automatically domestic goddesses, or they might not know the first thing about driving tractors and rearing lambs, so give genuine compliments when they are earned.

At least farmers have a good reputation for not giving false flattery, but the same extends to the giving of compliments so make an effort. However, don't overdo it: if Brian says "that's a lovely dinner" three or more times during the meal, the compliments seem to reinforce that he isn't overly impressed by my cooking on most other days.

You can't make a silk purse out of a sow's ear.

You can't create a good product from inferior materials – you could be talking about a material good or a person. I imagine the odd mother-in-law might have used this expression on occasion.

HOW TO MAKE TIME FOR DATE NIGHTS AND DAYS

All work and no play make Jack and Jill very dull people who argue because they have nothing else to talk about!

I know, taking time off is subject to permission from the cows, the sheep, the crops and the weather, but we farmers do have the advantage of not having to wait until the weekend to do something nice, so take the occasional midweek day off. In Ireland, the Office of Public Works gives free entry into all of their castles and gardens on the first Wednesday of every month, so you can combine some culture and history with a good day out without spending a small fortune.

It's easy to think the grass is greener on the other side and while you'll enjoy time away from the farm, trips to the big smoke will also make you realise just how lucky you are. Maybe the next date night could be a walk across the fields on a beautifully starry night.

The work will still be there when you get back, no one will have stolen it (unfortunately), but a few hours off together will gain a lot of brownie points *and* give you a breather.

Show her how much the farm means to you: share the stories about your ancestors, show her your plans, present the financial projections in a best case and a worst case scenario and make her feel part of the business. That way, she won't mind sacrificing for it; well, at least not too often.

Time for whom?

Social interaction is important. Whether you're nattering with other farmers at the co-op or chatting to a farm rep for an hour, it's good to talk. However, if that puts you under pressure for the rest of the day and you're using the other person as the reason for being late or not having time to spend with the kids, it will drive her insane. Chat away, but make family time too.

Okay, you're not away every Saturday playing golf, which is a plus, but do some stuff together and show an interest in each other's hobbies. If she's not from a farming background, she won't know what to do to help out so involve her in the farm and let her know what's going on. Save the "nice" jobs for when she's around at the weekends so you can have fun together doing them. Otherwise, it's all too easy for there to be a separation of the ways.

Include your wife

If you have one of those extended families who get together often and put the world to rights chatting about who sold land, who got married, who died, who was left what in a will, who harvested their corn last week, who bought a new car ... well, if she doesn't know any of these people the conversation is going to be as interesting as watching paint dry. She could bring a newspaper or magazine to flick through while listening with one ear but she's still going to be bored and feeling left out. (When I was a child, I always brought a book with me when visiting relatives. Unfortunately, adults can't really do that.)

Include her in the conversation by explaining who these people are and why the information is so interesting otherwise she is going to feel like an unwelcome outsider and will dread each get-together.

Remember farm women don't have to think too hard about how to take revenge if you've got on her nerves. She may decide to feed your tea to the dog. She might "borrow" your favourite jumper and it becomes hers for evermore. While other women might borrow a partner's razor to shave their legs, farm women might "borrow" your beard trimmer to shave the udders of their goats or show cows. So consider that before you start an argument!

And if the worse comes to the worse, there's always plenty of time to make up afterwards.

> #NeverSay
>
> "What have you been doing all day?"

HOW TO PREVENT A DIVORCE – DON'T GET MAD

Whether she is from a farming background or not, she'll be accustomed to doing things differently. Living with your wife is very different to living with your mother so don't get mad if any of the following occur:

◢ The grass has been cut for silage and the heavens have opened. She tries to say something comforting like "the forecast says it will be fine at the weekend". However, this is Monday. Don't blow a gasket: she means well.

◢ If she washed your clothes but forgot to empty your pockets. Just try to dry out the receipts on a radiator.

◢ If she goes for coffee with a friend instead of coming straight home with the veterinary products you asked her to collect – you should have told her that you needed them urgently.

◢ If she doesn't wash and dry your coat in one night like your mother used to. (Your mother used to get it washed and spun before she went to bed and then hung it near to the wood burning stove all night.)

◢ If she doesn't cook extra so there isn't "another dinner in the pot" when a sales rep arrives at dinner time.

⫟ If she decides to grow vegetables in your huge garden and on succeeding to grow hundreds of courgettes you're faced with having courgettes for every meal: tomato and courgette risotto, courgette and bacon pasta, courgette and meatballs, courgette and potato soup, courgette cake ... well, at least there's cake. She's delighted with her efforts so you're going to have to grin and bear it (and provide compliments). Maybe suggest she gives some courgettes to neighbours as a way of getting to know them better.

⫟ If she is more cautious than you about borrowing large sums of money and gets nervous seeing all those zeros.

⫟ If she doesn't mend your multiple pairs of torn trousers with patches – just hand them to your mother to repair. Your wife won't mind, honest.

⫟ If she volunteers you for a committee and then you have to attend meetings regularly.

⫟ If she gets cross when you tiptoe across the kitchen in your boots and makes you wash the kitchen floor.

⫟ If she makes a perfect latte but can't make a decent cup of tea as she forgets to scald the teapot each time.

⫟ If she gets rid of your favourite old (albeit stained and torn) armchair.

⫟ If you invite someone in for a cup of tea and there are no cakes baked.

⫟ If she can't forge your signature – change it to a squiggle!

⫟ If she spends money before the cattle are sold; she doesn't realise your superstition regarding not counting chickens before they are hatched.

Don't count your chickens before they are hatched.

Never presume anything; make sure the money is in the bank before you think about spending it.

HOW TO PAY HER COMPLIMENTS YOU REALLY MEAN

Why are compliments important? According to psychologist Maureen Gaffney, we need three positive experiences for every negative to stay well and manage our lives in an average way. Five positive experiences to one negative means we'll have the confidence and self-esteem to flourish. (Although don't go overboard; 11:1 means we're in denial and that's not healthy either).[62] A positive experience can be as simple as someone giving us a genuine compliment.

You have to be careful how you phrase your compliments because it could inadvertently sound like an insult. I cringe when I hear people say "You look great, you've lost loads of weight haven't you?" What they have effectively said is, "You were jolly fat the last time I saw you," in a not very complimentary way. Just tell them they look wonderful in that dress/jacket/trousers and leave it at that. (While we are on the topic of weight, never ever ask a woman if she is pregnant unless you've definitely heard that she is or she's actually in labour in front of you.)

What should you compliment her for? Sometimes you have to look for opportunities such as a haircut – that's an obvious one isn't it? Don't go on about how expensive it is just because you are almost bald and use a razor once a month.

Compliment her for what she does on the farm but also on how she looks. There will be days that she will feel less than glamorous, when her nail varnish is chipped, her hair needs to be cut and she has hay seeds tickling from inside her bra and yet she will never look more beautiful to you, so ensure you tell her. It's also important to compliment her when you go out on a proper date, when she's dressed up, wearing high heels and her eyes are sparkling with anticipation of some night life and some non-farm-related conversation. You might receive some praise in return too!

Admittedly some women aren't the best at receiving compliments. You admire her hair and she says she hasn't washed it for three days. You admire what she is wearing and you hear back "Oh, this old thing". After a while, you might feel what's the point in making flattering remarks? It works the other way too. If you shrug off compliments, she will stop giving them. Both of you need to accept compliments graciously and with a smile.

I'm not saying you deserve a clap on the back every time you take out the rubbish or milk the cows. It is important though to acknowledge successes no matter how big or small. It might be finishing the lambing with a good percentage of live lambs, increasing the milk solids this year or getting an improved yield of grain. Accept the compliment and go out to celebrate. Give yourself one evening a month to feel proud of yourself, and don't worry, your head should still fit through that door. If it doesn't, she'll knock you back into shape.

#NeverSay

"Stand on this gate – it needs a bit of weight to close it."

HOW TO ENSURE YOU DON'T HAVE TO SORT LIVESTOCK ON YOUR OWN

I'd say it's happened at least once on every farm in the country that one person has stormed off and left the other(s) to finish sorting on their own. If there's just the two of you, you kinda need her to stick around and finish the job! Here's how:

- Tell her you love her before you start.

- Be organised and prepare the space well with sufficient gates as barriers. Spending ten minutes beforehand setting up gates could save an hour later if things go amiss.

- If you are dividing livestock into two groups, for example, male and female calves, and you have to dose them beforehand, spray each male with a coloured dot when in the crush. The person in the gap just has to turn back all the dotted ones then.

- Give clear and concise instructions. Telepathy never works as it should in these situations.

- Don't swear. Some women up and leave the second they hear a curse as they know it signals the start of a rant.

- Don't expect her to be in two places at once.

⌐ Don't blame her if you end up making a pig's ear of it by confusing things and giving her incorrect information.

⌐ Don't blame her for everything that goes wrong. After all, she was at the other end of the crush when that cow went down.

⌐ Unless it's an emergency, don't shout.

⌐ Give her a hug at the end.

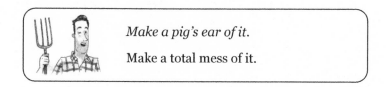

Make a pig's ear of it.

Make a total mess of it.

HOW TO BUY HER THE RIGHT GIFT

Gift buying can be a nightmare if you don't know what you're doing. It's difficult to choose a book that an avid reader hasn't read yet. Which bracelet do you choose? What size and style in clothing? She buys you a shirt and jumper every Christmas and you always love it, but it seems to be much more difficult the other way round.

Many farmers get their wives to buy the gifts and cards for all the other family members (which counts as housework, by the way) but you can't get away with letting her buy her own gift. Well, maybe you can but it's not going to be a nice surprise is it?

What's her favourite shop? No, don't buy her a gift voucher for it, although that is one option. Find out the name of the sales assistant she likes best and ask her what your wife would like. Let her advise you and wrap it up and all you have to do is pass over the credit card.

Of course, what will happen after a while is the sales assistant and your wife become best friends and plan her birthday and Christmas gifts so your gifts aren't surprises any more, but at least you're getting her a perfect present every time.

HOW TO GET AWAY ON A HOLIDAY

Everyone needs a break. It's not just about getting a physical rest; it's also about rekindling your enthusiasm and enabling you to think "outside the box". It's really important the whole family gets a break together. The children get to see a very different you. Recently, we've gone on lazy sun holidays and while we do activities like cycling, there's also lots of time for reading and relaxing. When the children saw Brian reading novels, they were so surprised; they must have thought we were chalk and cheese: he a philistine and me a bookworm.

There's no doubt about it, it can be difficult to get away on holidays when you're farming. If you work in partnership with others, it makes it easier but for most of us, we're on our own.

How to get away:

- ◢ Go at the quietest time of your farming year. We go in late January when the cows are dry before calving. This cuts down on the cost of farming labour as we don't have to get a relief milker.

- ◢ Some couples take holidays separately: she goes away with a good friend or a sister and he goes on a farming tour. That way, there isn't a problem with getting a relief worker and they both get a break. But wouldn't it be nicer to go away together?

- If you don't have a farm worker, ask a dependable neighbour or a contractor to feed your stock and keep an eye on things when you're away.

- If you find it takes you two days to unwind as you're still thinking about the farm, go to a different climate. The contrast in temperatures and scenery will help you forget about home.

- Leave instructions that you are not to be contacted if anything goes wrong as there's nothing you can do about it. Getting a call from a neighbour to tell you that your cows are on the road might be a tad stressful!

- Check your mobile phone only twice a day (just in case there's an emergency).

- Do not bring any farming literature on holidays with you!

- If you really start showing signs of withdrawal while you're away, go to a local mart to see how they do it differently.

- If both of you really want to live and breathe farming 52 weeks of the year, go on an agricultural holiday in another country where you visit lots of different farms as part of a guided tour.

Till the cows come home.

You'll have a long wait; indeed, it might never happen.

HOW TO COPE WHEN YOUR WIFE IS ILL

I know you're not allowed to have man flu but that doesn't mean your wife won't get sick occasionally. Be it flu, morning sickness or a common cold, you need to look after her.

- Don't presume she will be fine and leave her from morning until night. Call in and check if she needs things like paracetamol, DVDs, a cup of tea, a hot-water bottle …

- If you set a breakfast tray, make it look appetising. A teacup and saucer is going to be more manageable than a mug. Cut toast into soldiers.

- Go to the local shop and buy a bottle of Lucozade or 7Up.[63] It cured us when we were children so it should still work.

- If she decides she needs to see a doctor, drive her there.

- If you have young children, get your mum to look after them if you can't have them on the farm.

- Above all, make sympathetic noises, for one day at least.

> #NeverSay
> "Who's going to do the paperwork?" or
> "Do you think you'll be able to cook for the contractors next week?"

HOW TO MANAGE PAPERWORK

There are a lot of different responsibilities on a farm. A farm business requires a bookkeeper, an accountant, a taxi service, a veterinary surgeon, a cook, a baker, a mechanic, a tractor driver, a herdsperson, a milker, a negotiator, a seller, a buyer, a manager, an IT specialist, a content creator for social media and a midwife. And while you might be described as a Jack of all trades, you have to be an expert in most too.

Life is pretty busy if you're trying to do all of these tasks on your own, let alone be good at all of them. As you might expect, the veterinary surgeon and accountant are usually outsourced, but that's not to say farmers don't apply their own knowledge to sick animals or to managing their cash flow. It's up to the two of you to decide how to share the different roles. I know of family farms where she milks the cows and operates the dairy side of the business while he manages the arable. Who is going to manage the paperwork? It's one of the most important aspects of running a successful business and just throwing everything in the biggest shoebox you can find isn't going to cut the mustard unfortunately. As I have discovered!

#NeverSay
"Did you see that piece of paper I left on the table? I had written some numbers on it; I left it there only last week. You didn't throw it out, did you?"

In an ideal world, one or both of you will:

◢ File all paperwork once a week.

◢ Pin those important scraps of paper to the notice board rather than leaving them at the end of the kitchen table.

◢ Have an official office (not the end of the kitchen table).

◢ Use the farming apps for recording data. (Don't just download them and expect them to do it all on their own.)

◢ Decide if it really is beneficial to be registered for VAT (as it adds a lot of extra paperwork, not to mention the gnashing of teeth).

◢ Get an accountant who calls to your house at breakfast or elevenses time so both of you can see him/her. Much handier than having to head off to town.

◢ Get the accountant to call once every three months so bookwork is kept up to date and you're more informed about your finances.

◢ See your accountant at the end of each year so you know exactly what the tax bill will be in ten months' time.

◢ Have an accountant who speaks plain English.

Why does keeping the paperwork in order help you to stay married? Well, have you ever spent a couple of hours looking for an important piece of paper and not known whether to kiss or kill each other when it's finally turned up? We have and believe me, there are nicer ways to spend time together!

HOW TO APPRECIATE EATING WELL

Do you appreciate getting home-cooked dinners on a daily basis or do you take it for granted?

I know you live too far from town to order takeaways (unless you don't mind eating them cold), but the reality is home-cooked-from-scratch meals are becoming rare in some households. Only half of all meals consumed are cooked from scratch and less than 30 minutes is spent preparing the average dinner.[64] Apparently 10% of Irish people cook a meal from scratch only once a week, 26% buy ready-to-cook meals and 29% order takeaways on weekday evenings.[65] Lots of couples and families regularly eat takeaway meals, frozen pizzas, pre-prepared vegetables and ready meals.

You might think that being a farmer keeps you fit and healthy but apparently there are lots of obese farmers risking heart attacks out there.

Eating healthy meals is important.

#NeverSay
"I'm sure Mum could show you how to make it."

So if you get a home-cooked meal most days, you are one of the lucky ones. Instead of taking it for granted:

♪ Thank the cook for your meal, even if you sense there wasn't a lot of love put into making it on a particular day.

♪ Compliment your wife's cooking or she will think you prefer your mother's meals, become disillusioned and stop making an effort.

♪ Don't treat it as the end of the world if she forgets to put the sugar in a rhubarb tart – worse could have happened.

♪ Be thankful for your wife's choices. Don't ask her to cook the same meals as your mother did. She might be happy to get recipes or lessons from your mum but leave that decision to her.

♪ Text her in good time (well, as soon as you know) if you are going to be late. It limits the chances of dinner being burnt, dried up or given to the dog.

♪ Get stuck in too. If you don't know how to cook, ask for a lesson in cooking a simple meal. Cooking together is fun.

♪ Try the pasta and rice meals – they make a change from meat and spuds and you just might end up loving them. Variety is the spice of life after all.

♪ Clear off the table after the meal. Don't just sit there and expect to be waited on – unless you have a toddler or baby on your knee of course.

♪ Recognise that it is clever organisation and thriftiness, not laziness, to cook double amounts and either freeze half or keep the leftovers for the next day.

> Remember: A man who makes jokes about a woman in the kitchen stays single.

HOUSEHOLD IMPLEMENTS
ON THE FARM

If you want to infuriate your other half, just borrow something from the kitchen without telling her or forget to replace it. She will go to the cupboard or drawer, expecting her sewing scissors or sharpest knife to be there, spend ages looking for it and eventually discover you removed it for an "emergency". Surprise, surprise, you haven't replaced it. To save you from her ire and to keep you in her good books, here is a list for the supplies you should have in the farm stock cupboard:

- Cheap coffee – If a vet asks for coffee to treat a cow with a displaced abomasum, she doesn't mean your wife's favourite and expensive coffee. Keep a jar of relatively cheap instant coffee to hand for these emergencies.

- Washing-up liquid – This is used as a lubricant for checking the progression of cows, sheep or goats when giving birth. She won't want the bottle back so buy your own supply.

- Bread soda – She's not going to be happy when she's in the middle of making brown bread and discovers you have taken the entire container of bread soda to treat calves with bloat.

◢ Sharp knives – Yes, she buys you a penknife every Christmas but somehow it always goes missing. Admit it, you nip in and borrow a sharp knife from the kitchen while you're waiting for the penknife to turn up, don't you? What happens next? You forget to bring it back in and she finds half her best steak knives rusting in the shed. Buy yourself a couple of spare (cheap) penknives.

◢ Measuring cups or jug – When you need a measuring cup or jug to measure milk replacer for calves or lambs or to measure out sprays, taking one from a set of branded jugs or measuring cups will be obvious so she will never ever forget your betrayal. Yes, I know you have every intention of returning it when you're finished with it. Somehow it gets caught up in an empty bag or buried in some straw. If you see a flash of pink when you're cleaning out the shed, you can rightfully assume that she won't want it back.

◢ Honey – Honey works well for persuading a stubborn calf to drink milk from the bottle – put a couple of big spoonfuls into the milk and drizzle some over the teat. It's best to put a couple of spoonfuls into a disposable container rather than bringing out the whole jar.

◢ A strong hand-whisk – Taking the one from the set on the worktop to mix up the calf milk replacer is not a good idea. You might find yourself buying a whole new set for the kitchen and hearing a suggestion as to what you can do with the pasta spoon from the old set.

◢ Funnel - A funnel is handy for pouring milk into a bottle or petrol into the chainsaw. It is also handy for pouring salt into the dishwasher so get your own funnel!

◢ Sweeping brush – You've lost your broom and borrow the kitchen brush to sweep up cattle feed or dirty straw in the shed, but the thing is, once you've swept those things, she's not going to want that brush back into the house to sweep her kitchen floor. Therefore, you're not borrowing it but taking it – permanently.

⬩ Towels – Have a supply of old towels, specifically purchased cheap towels or old clothes as rags for the yard. They are handy for drying off a calf or lamb, wiping up blood or drying oily hands. Do not dash to the hot press/airing cupboard and grab the first bundle of towels you come across. If they are the soft cream ones she keeps for visitors, you are dead. Get "farm" towels in a dark red or mustard colour; make sure they are all the same, and totally different to any of the family towels. Oh, and don't throw them in the wash with the house towels.

⬩ Hairdryer – If you show livestock on a regular basis, you probably have your own set of grooming tools, but racing in to borrow her hairdryer and then leaving it on the ground is not going to go down well. Farmers have been known to borrow a hairdryer to defrost a frozen pipe too. Get your own, or bring the house one back immediately!

⬩ Vegetable oil – You know you use this if an animal has bloat so add it to your shopping list. Grabbing a bottle from the kitchen and then leaving it open outside where any kind of bug can get in isn't going to convince her to use it again. Heaven help you if the bottle you grabbed was an expensive bottle of organic unrefined extra virgin hand-pressed olive oil with herbs.

⬩ Scissors – Hell hath no fury like a woman missing her sewing scissors. Buying about six pairs of scissors is a good investment. You can never have too many.

⬩ Containers – Taking her Tupperware containers for storing items like ear tags or small tools isn't going to go down too well. Recycle ice-cream tubs and use them.

If, on the other hand, you find that she borrows your tools occasionally, buy her a set that is easily distinguishable from yours, perhaps a set with pink handles. If you see her using any in another colour, you know you can get your own back! Don't buy them as main Christmas or birthday presents though, just a little extra!

HOW TO ENSURE YOUR WIFE AND YOUR MOTHER GET ON

Your mother and your wife are the two most important women in your life and, naturally, you'd like them to get on well. The ideal situation, of course, is that your mother loves your wife to bits. She may be the daughter she never had or she's delighted to have another one. She's excited at the prospect of grandchildren, of seeing another generation born into the farm and she's overjoyed to see you both so happy. Ideally your wife is looking forward to learning about farming life from your mother. However, we don't live in an ideal world ...

Harridans in the past: myth or reality?

Mothers-in-law are commonly stereotyped as being nosy, interfering, domineering and maybe even spiteful. Is this a construct from television programmes or are they really like that? Do most mothers want to get on with their daughter-in-law? Are they delighted the wedding has happened? Or are they pretending to be happy but inside are they seething?

In the past, most new brides shared the farmhouse with their husband's family, sometimes just her mother-in-law, which was like setting a cat among the pigeons. According to Lisdoonvarna matchmaker Willie Daly:

> The groom's mother might in reality be about to turn into a real demon of a mother-in-law, but even she'd be in good spirits that night because her son had got himself a bride, and she could see the possibility of an heir to the throne if you like. But oftentimes beneath the smiles she would be desperately jealous towards the new wife. Oh, there'd be an awful lot of jealousy in the house. All of a sudden it was like an old car being replaced by a new one. The mother-in-law could see that she was about to be left aside, that her position of power was under threat, but she would fight her redundancy very hard and be a very devil. Not in all cases, mind you, but more often than not.[66]

In many ways, it was understandable. The older woman had probably lived under the thumb of her own mother-in-law. She may have worked hard on the farm, receiving a pittance in housekeeping money with no control or say in the finances. Or she may have been a domineering matriarch. Either way, she wouldn't have wanted to relinquish her status to this "young wan" coming in with her notions of piped water, electricity and a washing machine. Somewhat ironically, it seems a woman who'd had an awful time of it from her own mother-in-law in turn doled out harsh treatment to her daughter-in-law.

Did it really have to be like that? Well, when you compare it to animals, remember they will physically fight to establish a pecking order. Every year, as we put pregnant cows nearing their due date into the maternity unit, the ones already there fight with the newcomers. They head butt each other and can get very aggressive as they fight for dominance. So in some ways, I guess it's normal that one woman wants to be in charge.

For those who shared kitchens and got on well, it seems the younger woman accepted a "daughter" role and let the older woman retain control and her "queen bee" status.

Don't worry, some women get on very well. It's just when they are living too close together that challenges to peace and tranquillity can emerge. Every woman wants her own space in her house. Even my daughter, aged 12, likes to have the kitchen to herself when she's baking and I get out of the way.

Who wore the trousers?

Farm wives are historically portrayed as having to put up with a lot (i.e. husbands who drank excessively or who weren't good businessmen). Many women had hundreds of hens, milked cows and made butter to earn enough to rear a large family. Some were widowed young and kept the farm going. Farm wives were credited with being the backbone to Irish farming. "She's a great one to work" or "She kept the place going" were expressions frequently used to acknowledge the hard work of the woman and the uselessness of her husband.

Your mother may have appeared to say "yes, yes, yes" to your father's suggestions all those years. Did you ever consider that she planted the seeds for those ideas and let him think they came from his own brain? He may have signed up to something when a salesman came to the door; your mother might have cancelled the direct debits the following week and your father never realised. This isn't isolated to just your parents' generation. In 1944, an article in the *Sunday Independent* stated "The woman who can't make her husband in the long run do what she wants him to do is not a social problem – she is a case for a psychiatrist".[67] You have to appreciate the power of the female in the household.

You also need to be very cautious in case the two of them (your wife and your mother) join forces and gang up on you. You wouldn't have a hope!

The mother-in-law now

Now you are married, your mother has become a mother-in-law. Will she metamorphose from your loving mum into an authoritarian mother-in-law overnight? Of course not. I think the vast majority of mothers want to get on well with their daughter or son-in-law, and can be of great help to the younger couple: sharing expertise, looking after grandchildren, and giving the husband meals if his wife is working off-farm.

But there are things that can throw a spanner in the works so it is best to be aware of them.

If your mum is the typical Irish Mammy, no woman will ever be good enough for you. It doesn't matter if your wife comes from the best farming stock, knows how to calve a cow and is a qualified accountant. It's not enough that she has won baking prizes at county shows, can drive a tractor and run fast enough to turn around escaping animals. Your mother will tell the neighbours about her wonderful daughter-in-law but can still find some flaws.

Alternatively, your mother might think she is too good for you. If so, she worries she will tire of you or suspect she's after the road frontage and half the farm. She might be celebrating outwardly that you've managed to meet such a wonderful woman at long last but she might also be worried sick you won't be able to keep her. She'll be watching her like a hawk for signs of boredom or dissatisfaction, waiting for the moment when she ups and leaves and she can say "I knew it, I told Mary I knew it would never last ..."

How to help them get on

It is natural the two of them have very different ways of doing things. Here are some examples to help you understand. Both will see their way as "the right way and the only way".

Your mother	Your wife
Was a full-time farm wife and domestic goddess but didn't necessarily do much farm work, was on numerous committees	Works full-time off-farm, is planning a farm diversification business, does all the paperwork. Can milk cows, feed calves and stand in a gap as required. No time for meetings
Puts clothes pegs in a bag when not in use	Leaves clothes pegs on the line, not worrying if they become brittle
Inspects for rain clouds when clothes are on the line	If the clothes get wet they'll dry some other time
Hangs trousers on the clothes line by the waistband	Hangs trousers on the clothes line in no particular way
Makes the Christmas puddings and cake in August	Decides in December to buy baked goods in M&S
Dinner is served at exactly 1pm each day	Dinner time fluctuates but everyone is fed eventually
Farm clothes are ironed	Farm clothes *may* be folded
Holey socks are darned	Holey socks are thrown out
Leaves the kitchen spotless every night, washing up whatever won't fit in the dishwasher	Hopes the fairies come during the night, but if not, the dirty dishes remaining can go in the dishwasher in the morning
Bakes every day – bread, cakes, tarts or scones	Bakes once a week. Hopes *this time* they last the week
Always has an extra dinner in the pot	Is left scrambling when an unexpected contractor turns up
Insists on the regular farm reps going in for a cup of tea and a scone when they call	Hopes the farm reps stay up the yard as she's busy
Has matching tableware	Hmmm, tried that but someone brought the mugs to the field one night for the contractors' tea

It's very easy to stick your head in the sand and ignore any ripples of discontent or presume a disagreement will blow over. Here are some tips to ensure discord doesn't happen. You don't want to be stuck in the middle; you want an easy life!

Never choose favourites

Don't – ever – play one off against the other and never ever choose the cooking of one over the other. You have to eat an equal amount of each person's home-made dishes, whether you are at a family meal or a community fundraiser. If each of them makes a dessert, you need to eat a portion of both. The same goes for any dish – even if the two of them make a potato salad, pile a large spoonful of each onto your plate.

Prove you're well looked after

You are the apple of your mother's eye and sometimes she might think your wife doesn't take sufficient care of you. If your mum has mollycoddled you for years, ironed your clothes, made you cups of tea, cooked, baked, ensured you're never hungry, she might consider your wife is lacking if she doesn't cook you a three-course meal every day. Therefore, you have to prove you are healthy and well-nourished but not being overfed, so stay fit and don't put on weight. You need to keep the side up.

Carefully select living accommodation

If you build a second house on the farm, put some distance between the two houses for both their sakes. The most important criteria are they can't see each other's front doors, visitors' cars or clothes lines. If your mother's life has changed from being very busy on the farm to having lots of free time and yet she doesn't leave the farm very often, her interest may focus on the comings and goings of your family, and in particular your wife. Building a Berlin wall between the two houses is another option. It's not necessarily easy, but it will be quicker to just have a word.

Don't be useless

Can you iron a shirt? Put on a load of washing? Empty the dishwasher? Find the laundry basket? Cook a meal? Wash the kitchen floor? If yes, you owe your mother a great debt. If not, you are going to have to learn – fast.

You have to be an Ideal Farm Husband; otherwise you're letting your mother down as your wife will blame her. You see, since the mid twentieth century (and perhaps before), it was believed that if a farmer is bad-mannered, useless or selfish, the main fault lies with his mother. The *Sunday Independent* even warned women that if they have criticisms about their husbands (and are blaming their mothers-in-law), they must make sure their own daughters-in-law won't have the same grievances.[68] Therefore, you can't have your wife thinking that you're hopeless when it comes to household chores. She will only hold your mother accountable for your failings in domesticity. Admit you need some help and get her to show you.

If you get your mum to give you tips at this late stage in your life, she might think it's awful that you have to do it. Of course, there is the chance she is very proud of you and wishes her husband had acted like that.

Knock knock. Who's there?

Mothers and other members of the groom's family might pop into the house at any time, unannounced. This is especially likely if the newlyweds are living in the original family home. Siblings might come home for holidays and expect to stay there while your wife cooks and cleans for them.

I've heard of mothers-in-law going in when the house is empty and re-arranging things or doing some cleaning. I know most of us wait in vain for fairies to tidy the kitchen at night and it would be lovely to have someone clean our houses. However, it's a different ball game if someone does it without permission and because it's apparently not done well enough. Your wife may be amused at first; she may even be grateful at times, but if it goes on too long, she'll get really annoyed.

Before it becomes a big argument between them, it's your job to gently break the news to your family that it isn't their house any longer, and while they are very welcome on occasion, you both need your space and privacy. Be firm from day one – it makes it easier in the long run.

Be loyal

Never complain about your wife. So what if her home-made brown bread was a tad clammy in the middle? Just toast those slices and slather them with butter and jam.

It's perfectly normal for women to have different standards regarding cleanliness. If your mother is fastidious about cleaning and your wife prefers to spend time reading a book or playing with the kids than dusting, then you have a choice. You must either help your wife clean before your mother arrives and does the white-glove test, or make it clear to your mum that you find it more relaxing to live in a house that's allowed to get a bit untidy. Just don't reveal you have sore knees from scrubbing the kitchen floor or that you've a sore foot after stepping on a piece of Lego that morning.

Your mother may suspect that you're not being looked after in the way in which you were accustomed but she won't have any evidence!

Spend time with them separately

Don't be pulled between the two of them or it might send you over the edge trying to keep them both happy. You need your own "me time" too, so be firm. If your wife knows she is number one, she won't begrudge you spending some time with your mum. If your wife is working off-farm and you get your dinner at your mum's house, it makes it easier to divide your time. Just don't let yourself be monopolised.

Things you must never say

> #NeverSay
>
> "My mother always did it like ..."
> "My mother used to ..."
> "My mother never ..."

Brian occasionally says things like "My mother would never have gone to bed leaving dirty dishes in the kitchen", or "My mother swept the floor four times a day" in the hope that I might become more domesticated. I could take it as criticism that I'm not living up to certain standards, but I never do. Aside from hitting him over the head with something, I find it quite funny that he is still trying to resign himself to living in a household that will never be as orderly as his childhood one. Do I try to change? No. I take it all with a liberal pinch of salt and pass him the sweeping brush. However, some women try really hard to create a good impression so comments like that, especially in the early stages of marriage, will do more harm than good.

It's all in the preparation. Start the way you mean to go on. However, you must appreciate that if they don't get on and you're trying to keep them both happy, you'll be walking on a tightrope and will just add to your stress levels. Your mum has to know you will always think she's the best mum in the world but you've got to prioritise your own spouse and children now. Your wife and children have to feel they come first in your life – to your parents, to your siblings, to your livestock, to the crops. If you do that, everyone will get along much better!

Here's to a long and happy life together, as husband, wife and mother-in-law.

How to get on with your own mother-in-law

It's always presumed the wife's mother is perfect, and she may well be. However, all mothers have a habit of believing they can be as involved in your life when you're 35 as when you were 15. It can be hard for mums to learn to back off. Her mother may help out with childcare especially when the children are small. It's wonderful for your wife to have extra help, especially with a new baby, but if you find yourself nearly having to ask permission for a chance to hold your child, you're bound to feel a bit put out. The baby won't break if you're not holding it exactly right so give yourself time to get used to being a dad.

If your mother-in-law comes to stay, you can catch up on lots of jobs, but if you find yourself regularly working outside till 11pm and it's not harvest or calving season, you know it's affecting you. Like the situation above when you had to say something to your family, you need to explain how you feel to your wife and ask her to take some action. Remember though, she'll only do so if you do it too.

And to get into the good books, don't forget that in addition to Mother's Day, there's now a Mother-in-law Day to celebrate your relationship with her. Yes, it's on the fourth Sunday of October. Be a wonderful son-in-law and put it in the diary now.

HOW TO REAR CHILDREN ON THE FARM

Growing up on a farm provides children with a wonderful upbringing. There were so many marvellous elements to farming that formed the highlights of our school holidays. Not everything we did was safe though so I wouldn't recommend some of them for children now! As some of these things came around only once a year, they created very special memories.

◢ Hay making – Between using bales as hurdles in obstacle courses, jumping off bales, travelling home on top of a load of bales, stopping for ice-cream on the way home and having picnics in the hay field, the haymaking season held one delight after another.

◢ Trailer rides – You wouldn't let a child do it now (which is probably why trailer rides at agricultural shows are always such a hit) but we rode on empty trailers as well as sitting on top of loads of small square bales as the tractor trundled home.

◢ Old tyre swing – Even though the rim of the tyre chafed our legs and left a deep indentation, not to mention remnants of murky water inside splashing us, there was nothing like a tyre swing in a huge old tree.

- Making mud pies – Water, old sand and some old plastic remnants of a doll's tea set kept us entertained for many an afternoon as we served up mud pies to all and sundry.

- Climbing trees – I always felt a bit of a failure as I never managed to climb trees to the same heights as they did in Enid Blyton books, but I spent hours at a time in our woodland. I viewed it as enormous but it's really quite small.

- Building treehouses –An entire summer holiday could be devoted to accumulating old boards, branches and foliage to build a treehouse (which was often constructed on the ground). More fun was had by the building of it than when it was finished.

- Paddling, minnows and frogspawn – All a kid needs for a few hours' entertainment are a small flowing stream and a couple of containers plus a belief that their frogspawn would turn into frogs and their minnows into giant fish.

- Picking conkers – Even though the conkers weren't the type to be roasted, we still got great fun out of picking conkers, drilling a hole through them, tying on a string and trying to bash each other's. Such is the fame and enjoyment of this game, conker championships are still held in Kilkenny every October.

- Riding in the transport box – The transport box was carried on the back of the tractor, usually blue, and big enough to take a couple of small bales or milk churns. Many a bachelor farmer carried his sister and neighbours home in it from the bus or the local shop. Many a parent carried a few children in it between the home farm and the out-farm.

- Pets – Exotic pets in our childhood were limited to some hens that were different from the norm. Some families kept a goat as it was believed a goat running with cows would ward off disease. Finding farm kittens was always a highlight, as was the farm dog having pups.

⌐ Town cousins staying – Nearly every farm kid had town cousins who arrived for a fortnight's holiday. They were often half wild and had no common sense when it came to working with animals or machinery. It always took a couple of days to decide whether or not we liked each other and then by the end of the fortnight we were usually inseparable.

⌐ Pet lambs – Although parents were never too keen on a lot of pet lambs, for children they were a great novelty. Luckily, the novelty had usually worn off by the time the lambs had to go to market.

⌐ Travelling on the tractor – I can still remember the excitement when the Zetor tractor arrived. It has a passenger seat and wide mudguards over each tyre which served as comfortable seats – so much more child friendly than the narrow Massey Ferguson. Whenever our mum announced she was going to town, there was a clamour of "Dad, what are you doing?" Hours sitting on the tractor spreading fertiliser were far preferable to an afternoon around the shops.

Many of these experiences still exist for kids, although the legal position about children on machinery is much more stringent. In Ireland, children under seven are not allowed on a tractor, even on a passenger seat. Some things change but very special memories can still be created for children by:

⌐ Being snowed in, having days off school and building snowmen.

⌐ Tobogganing down a hilly field on sheets of galvanised iron or in a plastic sandpit box.

⌐ Playing hide and seek in a field of bales.

⌐ Picnics in the field.

⌐ Picking mushrooms and blackberries.

- Learning how to drive in a field (or tearing around in an old car).

- Staying up late when the silage is being harvested (and avoiding mum on each tractor run back to the yard).

- Going for a walk late at night across the fields when the moon is bright. This is special whether it's a balmy evening or there's snow on the ground.

What about work? Partly because farming was more labour intensive then but also because machinery wasn't available or was less powerful, children helped out on the farm from an earlier age and much more often. Jobs included:

- Stacking small square bales, loading them onto a trailer and then into the hay barn – lots of blisters!

- Weeding beet

- Picking potatoes

- Harvesting vegetables

- Feeding calves

- Collecting eggs and feeding hens

- Painting gates and fences

- Feeding pigs

- Hand-milking cows

- Going off on bikes to do the herding on the out-farm

- Bringing in the cows

- Making jam

- Baking

- Chopping firewood and bringing in sticks

- Going to the mart with cattle or sheep.

As farms become even more mechanised and machinery gets bigger, there are fewer jobs children can do. Our kids scrape out the cubicles as we don't have automatic scrapers and they help to feed the calves as we haven't automatic calf feeders, but if we modernise, some jobs will be going. They also bring in the cows to be milked and help with the milking.

While sheep farmers can get young children involved in bottle feeding pet lambs, suckler farmers find that the stock are too big and just not calm enough for young children to help out.

A farm gives children the scope to practise their entrepreneurial skills, be it selling eggs and garden produce at the gate and leaving an honesty box, showing livestock at agricultural shows or just bargaining for decent pocket money for the various farm jobs they do. Farm kids don't need to get paper rounds; most farms will have plenty for them to do once they become teenagers.

Six things to remember re safety:

- Ensure the children's playground is secure, or there is a gate between the garden and yard that they cannot open (or climb over).

- Set ground rules with them, perhaps the most important one being they cannot go up the yard unless an adult is with them.

- If older children are going around the farm on their own, tell them they must let you know what area or fields they will be in.

- Keep the shed with medicines, sprays and chemicals locked (as they should be in any case).

- Do a risk assessment regularly and explain all the safety signs to them.

- Don't overwork children or put them in situations where they may not have the experience to react quickly or appropriately to a threat.

Remember the best toys for children tend to be twine, dirt and a stick – and there are lots of those in a farmyard. Build a huge sandpit near the house and put a tonne of builders' sand into it. They'll get years of fun out of it.

In many ways, being brought up on the farm hasn't changed that much since you were a lad. Manure still stinks; going to an agricultural show is the highlight of the summer holidays, even now; farm kids still experience the hazard of falling into nettles. They learn how to work hard as there's always plenty to do; parents will always be late because a ewe was lambing or something got out, and they'll never get to open all their presents first thing on Christmas morning.

And Irish farmers can now get two weeks paternity leave. The €230 per week won't give you two full weeks off but it will go some way towards getting some help so you can spend extra time with your newborn. And don't think that dealing with animal excrement outside gets you out of nappy changes. If anything, you should be a dab hand at it.

HOW TO COPE WITH INFERTILITY

Infertility is tough for any couple and although it can feel it's only happening to you, it does affect more than one in six couples. Many people think those affected haven't any children but it can happen that those with one, two or more children can't conceive any more or experience numerous miscarriages and never find out the reason why.

Living on a farm doesn't make infertility any easier. There's the reminder of birth every calving or lambing season. There's the knowledge that animals that don't become pregnant are almost always culled, which doesn't exactly offer great encouragement to a woman who can't get pregnant or carry a baby to term. Infertile bulls are sent to the factory too, so you're not unaffected by this either. People always tend to ask if you have children. I presume this can be infuriating for couples who want to remain childless but it can be very hurtful, albeit unintentionally, for those who really want a family.

The vast majority of farmers would love if one of their children took over the farm someday. I don't think it's a good thing to force children to farm nor to presume they will do so, but for some, the farm can feel barren when there aren't any children around. Add a mother-in-law who really wants an heir and keeps going on about the pitter-patter of tiny feet and it can make an already sensitive situation worse.

So how can you cope with infertility without it tearing you up inside? Will it affect your partner more than it affects you? I'm not going to try and pretend I have the answers. Taking action helps. Explore all the options and don't say no to any of them until you've exhausted your research in fertility treatment, fostering, adoption or surrogacy.

Infertility can really test a relationship and it's by offering support, and seeking support for yourself too, that you'll both get through it.

QUIZ (FOR HER)

Let's assess if he is shaping up to be an Ideal Farm Husband.

1. What is the best thing about being married to a farmer?
    (a) Not having to pay gym membership.   ❏
    (b) Life is never boring.   ❏
    (c) Working alongside your best friend and spending
         lots of time together, knowing that you're a team.   ❏

2. When you want him to fix something in the house, what's the most effective way to get him to do it?
    (a) You eventually make a start on it yourself; sooner
         or later he will come along to watch and then take
         over. He'll finish it and claim all the credit.   ❏
    (b) You say: "If you don't have time, I'll ring Handy
         Andy and get him to do it." He has it done within
         the week.   ❏
    (c) You choose a time when he hasn't got any urgent
         work and he does it within a couple of days.   ❏

3. How does he help/share in the cooking?
   (a) He will come along when it is bubbling on the hob, taste, add a condiment, give it a stir and apparently he's cooked it. ❑
   (b) He eats it and gives you his opinion. ❑
   (c) He cooks Sunday lunch every week. ❑

4. How does he help with the housework?
   (a) He helps with washing the outside of the upstairs windows. He drives the digger to the house; you get into the bucket; he lifts it up and leaves you there, returning periodically to move the digger into position for the next window. ❑
   (b) He runs the hoover around the middle of the living room and thinks the place is done. ❑
   (c) He helps for two hours every Saturday morning so he can watch the rugby in peace in the afternoon. He even bought a steam mop for the kitchen floor. ❑

5. How do you know when he's really happy with life?
   (a) He chats to the sales reps for a lot longer. ❑
   (b) He whistles while he's working; he might even serenade the cows by singing lustily in the milking parlour. ❑
   (c) He suggests a good night out to celebrate a recent success. ❑

6. He's been working a long day and gets an irritated text from you because he's late for supper with the children again. Does he:
   (a) Get the hump, eat and go back out to work? ❑
   (b) Apologise; go to say goodnight to the kids before eating and fall asleep beside one of them? ❑
   (c) Sit at the table to eat, with children in pyjamas clambering all over him, then chase them up the stairs to read them a story in bed? ❑

7. The silage is being cut on your children's sports day. What does he do?
    (a) Gets you to video their races so he can watch it with them later. ❑
    (b) Gets in to watch their races for half an hour and makes sure the kids see him at the beginning and the end so they think he's there for longer. ❑
    (c) Reckons he is paying the contractors enough so after checking all is okay, he leaves them to it and goes in to watch the kids for the afternoon. ❑

8. When forced to wear holey trousers because all the non-holey pairs are in the wash, does he:
    (a) Say his mother would never have left them torn like that. ❑
    (b) Reckon he'd better be careful or everyone at the farm store will get an eyeful. ❑
    (c) Decide to demote a pair of good but old jeans to farm trousers? ❑

How did you do?
Mostly A's – Hmmm, he knows what he has to do, but he does need to put more effort in sometimes. He likes to claim the credit for a job well done. It's just a case of getting him to do more of those jobs.
Mostly B's – He has good intentions so that's half the battle.
Mostly C's – He's not perfect yet but he's very nearly there. Certainly an Ideal Farm Husband in the making.

PART SEVEN

YOUR HEALTH

ALIVE AND KICKING

An ideal farm husband needs to be energetic, diligent, resilient, passionate and contented. It helps if he's also a good communicator, an excellent negotiator and a hard worker. Farming is a challenging occupation in itself but not half as demanding as the people you come into contact with so this section is about ensuring that you're still alive and kicking after a couple of decades as a farmer.

HOW TO SURVIVE LONG WORKING HOURS

Working long hours in farming is normal life for most, but overly long hours can become harmful to your health and family life. If you're tired, you're not going to have the same reflexes or reaction time if an animal kicks out or a gate slams shut. Tiredness can lead to accidents and injury or worse. Long working hours can affect family relationships too and you know what they say about all work and no play making Jack a dull boy. You need recreation and rest to sparkle!

◢ Wouldn't it be lovely to be able to hibernate for a while before a really busy spell? The best you can do is go on holiday and psych yourself up for the two-month burst of calving, lambing, sowing or harvesting. Alternatively, have a good holiday planned for immediately afterwards. All turkey farmers should head off to the sunshine on 26 December.

◢ If there's too much work waiting on you, hire in help, be it a full-time permanent worker or a couple of students on a short-term basis. However, make sure they are good workers or it could end up causing you even more stress.

◢ If you can't afford extra labour, then you've no other option but to knuckle down and get on with it. Ask yourself "will doing this job make me money?" and that will determine the essential jobs. Let the frills go and have a very long finger for the non-essentials.

◢ Outsource work if you can by getting contractors to do some. For example, rather than buying a new dung spreader when the old one dies, consider getting the contractors to do that job in future.

◢ If you crave a good social life and like to go out a couple of evenings a week or if you're becoming overburdened with the amount of work, then it's up to you to make the decision to change things. Some dairy farmers have gone to once-a-day milking to reduce workload for example.

◢ If possible, plan your day so you manage to see the children when they come home from school and before bed. While your wife may take some time to adjust to being a "harvest widow", it'll make life easier for you if she's happy reading books or working on something of her own when you're working late.

◢ While advice from experts can often be very good, remember they are sitting in an office and go home at 5pm with a pay packet guaranteed every month, so sometimes you need a liberal pinch of salt to keep things in perspective.

◢ Ignore other people's way of doing things. Some people find their efficiency improves when they know they are finishing work at a certain time. Others find that too pressured and just concentrate on getting the task finished and whether its 6pm or 9pm, it doesn't matter but it will be finished. Work to whichever method suits your productivity and stress management.

◢ If you're dog-tired but not sleeping well, don't take risks driving when you're exhausted. It could be a good idea to visit the doctor.

Depression or emotional burnout from overwork and financial stress are very real. You won't be the first, nor the last, farmer to experience them. It's vital that your family life is as healthy as it possibly can be as you'll need their support. Don't take your stress out on the family. It's not their fault and they are doing what they can to help you on the farm. It's vital that everyone pulls together to get through a tough time but don't forget to celebrate when it's all over.

Oh, and store up all that irritability until you experience some really bad customer service someday and let them know all about it! As long as you don't go overboard with a rant, it can be quite satisfying.

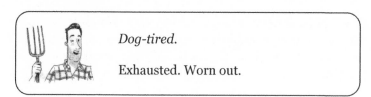

Dog-tired.

Exhausted. Worn out.

HOW TO GET A QUICK POWER NAP

Power naps are the best thing ever when you're tired. A 20-minute nap is often enough to give you energy to keep going for a few more hours (but this works only on a short-term basis!). Any longer than 20 minutes and you're liable to feel very groggy when you wake up. Don't go to bed! Move to a relatively comfortable armchair after dinner and have a quick nap. Stop the tractor in the field and sleep for ten minutes.

If you're out for the night to the theatre or the cinema, you should manage a 15-minute nap without anyone noticing as long as you don't snore. I seem to sleep for about 20 minutes whenever I bring the children to the cinema. What about if you're out for dinner with friends? It's impossible to get a nap at a restaurant, but if visiting their home I suggest moving to a comfortable armchair and just dozing off for the few minutes. Your conversation will be much brighter when you wake. They will understand, and if they are farmers themselves they might even join you.

HOW TO YAWN WITHOUT PEOPLE NOTICING

Have you ever been in a situation when you're really tired or bored and you really want to yawn but you just can't?

If you're at a dinner table, you can pretend to let something fall and take a silent yawn under the table when you bend down to pick it up. Otherwise, you are limited to yawning with your mouth closed. You need to close your eyes and purse your lips together. Yes, you'll look like you are going to do the loudest sneeze ever but you won't have shown off your tonsils while you yawned.

HOW TO HANDLE BEING IRRITATED

Being exasperated by family, friends and neighbours is normal at some point or another. However, knowing how to react appropriately and let it all go over your head can make the irritation quite amusing instead of driving you to boiling point.

Common irritations

Trying to keep up with the Joneses is exhausting, expensive and irritating. Just because some neighbours got new cars or new tractors, it doesn't mean you need them. The farming media is often full of stories of farmers expanding and it may feel that the only way to farm properly is to increase scale. This usually means borrowing. But there's no point having a brand new tractor and struggling to fill it with diesel. Concentrate on what you're doing and do it well.

By the way, driving an old tractor or car on the road makes other drivers get out of the way as they are conscious your vehicle is worth much less and hence you mightn't drive with quite as much care as they do.

Farmers copying each other can be mildly annoying. One farmer will spread fertiliser and they all rush to get it out. If they don't manage to do so before the rain comes, they'll console themselves with "Ah, sure, his is washed down the river; at least I still have mine in the yard." Ask yourself if he's really spreading anything. It's not unknown for a farmer to go out with an empty fertiliser spreader as a joke, to see if others copy him.

When a calf stands on your foot, really really heavily – shouting and cursing helps slightly. It's called lalochezia – the use of vulgar language to relieve stress or pain. If your wife tells you to wash out your mouth with soap, just tell her the cursing is medicinal.

When a cow swishes her tail into your face, swear (yes, medicinal again), grab the shears and trim it. Otherwise, she'll do it again at the next milking.

When you're making yourself a cup of tea and there's hardly a drop of milk left in the fridge, you'll nearly feel like crying if you've milked a hundred cows and the milk lorry has just collected two days' worth of milk. Most people would nip to the shop but you'd never drink that watery stuff. You're going to have to drink black tea, but have lots of extra chocolate to compensate.

When neighbours don't keep good fences and one or two of their cattle get into your field repeatedly and they don't hurry to remove them, lock them (the cattle!) into a shed and your neighbour will soon come looking for them.

When cows take it in turn to calve all night, just as one calves, another starts to heave – all you can do is eat more chocolate and have a power nap. Or ask your beloved if she would take the middle of the night shift.

It's annoying when you can't escape your past. No matter what you do or how big your successes are, people will always remember the failures and mistakes from your past as well as those of your ancestors. It's been that way for years. HV Morton noticed it in the 1930s:

He will over a glass of porter tell you all about the local ancestors. He stands in Mike Finnigan's drink-shop brooding about parentage. He knows everything about everybody.

"D'ye see that man now?" he will ask, half turning from the saloon counter and pointing with his pipe to indicate a man in the street, "That's Paddy Milligan, the Sheep Stealer!"

"What?" you ask, surprised. "Does he steal sheep?"

A grim, condemnatory look will come into the man's face and he will tell you solemnly:

"Shure his grandfather was hanged for sheep stealing!"[69]

All you can do is the best you can and tell yourself they are only jealous.

It can be a tad annoying when non-farmers comment on the increase in milk/grain/meat prices as if you're now living in the land of milk and honey, yet never comment when the prices drop. On the other hand, they are probably less annoying than the begrudgers who don't acknowledge or congratulate you when you have a success.

When people tell you that you're really lucky to be farming but they are visiting on a warm sunny day when the livestock are out and the fields look nice and green – you know you are, but you can just picture them snuggling deeper under the duvet when it's freezing cold and lashing sleet on a winter's morning at 6am.

Some see dairy products as liquid gold and the dominant attitude is all other farmers must be simple if they aren't milking cows. All you have to do is wait for a year with bad milk prices for them to see sense! I'm afraid you never have to wait long.

When you are seen as a Luddite if you don't have the latest in new machinery and new technology, just smile when you see your bank statement and imagine what it would be like if you had a new tractor out in the yard.

Roaming dogs when you're a sheep farmer – enough said.

Drivers of cars who don't wave or flash to say thank you when you've pulled in on the tractor to let them pass. You can't not pull in as if you're caught with a long line of cars behind you, you'll get points on your licence and a fine. (Don't pull in to the hard shoulder on a dual carriageway unless there is something wrong: doing so could land you with a fine too.)

And if all else fails, use Mrs Brown's version of f*** off and just say "that's nice". It will make you feel so much better.

A red rag to a bull.

Deliberately provoke someone, knowing you'll get a reaction.

MANAGING STAFF

On many farms, the family are the staff except when contractors arrive occasionally. Sometimes, therein lies the problem. Where farms were busy places years ago between large families, labourers and the annual meitheal[70] at harvest time when neighbours came to help, farms tend to be quiet now as improved mechanisation means reduced labour.

It's interesting to examine how workers were hired and treated in the past. There was one hiring time a year. Labourers and servants went to a local fair looking for work for the year, bargaining with a farmer for wages and board. For many, the living conditions and food allowances were more important than the wages, which suggests some had very bad experiences. Sleeping in outside houses near cow byres or in lofts was common. According to Liam O'Donnell, while some labourers ate with the family, it was often that the "servant boy ate by himself in the kitchen while the boss and herself and family ate in the parlour, a special room away from the kitchen".[71]

On larger and more prosperous farms with plenty of workers, they seem to have been well fed and a strict timetable was adhered to. *The Farm by Lough Gur* is almost poetic in its descriptions, yet milk, bread and potatoes were the main foodstuffs.

For breakfast they [ploughmen and farm boys] had maizemeal stir-about with plenty of milk, sometimes potatoes; in later years home-made bread was added. Dinner was at 12.30, consisting of milk in "piggins" [a round wooden vessel] potatoes and dip; bacon was given twice a week. The men's tea was taken out to them at four o'clock, with bread and butter in great slices. The maids had the same food, but at different time, and for supper at 7:30 bread and milk, hot or cold, or porridge with plenty of sweet milk. On this simple fare maids and men throve; they were all healthy, hearty and good tempered.[72]

Farmers advertised in newspapers for staff too. Many farm workers worked in a particular industry be it milking cows, field work or with sheep. According to AG Street, many of their workers would have been insulted if asked to work at something else; for example, a shepherd would never milk cows and would only help out at the harvest if he really had to.[73] Farmers were quite specific in their advertising and it seems men were sought for field work, and youths and women to milk cows and look after livestock in the yard. Dairy farmers requiring milkers advertised for whole families.

Irish Examiner 4 March 1912
Wanted one or two farm labourers, one to plough, no milkers required, good terms to suitable men.

Wanted a family of farm labourers, one or two men, with wife or daughter to milk a few cows and care for fowl.

Milking cows was very much seen as women's work until mechanisation came in.

Some workers got their own cottages, complete with a plot to grow potatoes or graze a couple of sheep. Coal and milk were also provided.

Irish Examiner 4 March 1912

Farm labourer wanted from March 25th. Must be a good ploughman. Terms: house free; 9s weekly, potato garden, grass for sheep and coal.

Wanted one or two farm labourers, if two, father and son or brothers, one a ploughman, both able to milk; house, milk, quarter potato garden. Apply with references, stating wages.

Irish Examiner 13 August 1951

Farmer worker wanted: furnished house with hot and cold water and electricity available for capable, willing person. Clonakilty.

It's interesting a farm cottage had electricity and piped water in 1951 when many farmers' houses didn't have them until the late 60s and beyond. Now, of course, the vast majority of farm workers live off-farm unless they are students.

Hospitality has changed on farms too. Traditionally, all the neighbours who came to help at the harvest were given dinner, tea and refreshments. My dad had to leave a neighbour's early once as he knew he was going to be the only one milking the 14 cows. When they resumed work the next day, the neighbour told him to never do that again, that he should have gone to the house for tea before he left. This insistence on feeding workers and visitors is one of the reasons you can't get away with refusing a cup of tea and a slice of cake if offered to you. Nowadays though, farm wives often work off-farm during the day so aren't there to cook a midday meal. Workers either bring a sandwich or go home for their lunch if they live nearby.

If the scale of the farm is large enough to have workers, it means that you have company as well as someone reliable to take over when you're away on holidays. Just remember that there's no point in having a dog and doing the barking yourself.

For most farmers, the family are the staff! Working as a husband and wife team on the farm can be one of the reasons why the farming life is so wonderful. You have to be calm though. You can really turn a nice peaceful task like vaccinating cows together into a headache if you're impatient and irritable. Remember you're blessed to be able to spend your working life as well as leisure time with your family.

Don't keep a dog and bark yourself.

There is no point in hiring staff if you are unable to delegate and end up doing most of the jobs yourself.

HOW TO DEAL WITH SALES REPS

Sales representatives: annoying or hugely important? Both, really. Some will annoy. They might do daft things like:

- Wear inappropriate clothing such as a suit and shoes and look ridiculous as they try to avoid stepping in any muck.

- Arrive at mealtimes, which might be the only time in the day when the whole family are together for an hour.

- Hang around even though you're talking to another sales person.

- Arrive at any stage of the month rather than calling at approximately the same date each month so you know to expect them.

- Make you feel awkward or beholden when you can't afford to pay the full bill.

I think the best sales people are those who thank you for the order and say something along the lines of "any chance of a few pound this month", knowing you're going to be handing over a cheque for a few thousand.

The most annoying have to be those who drive into the yard and beep the horn as if summoning you. Send them off with a flea in their ear. If, on the other hand, your wife beeps the horn, run. Not away from her! Towards the car as the beeping means she's in a hurry and needs you Right Now.

Salespeople are important in other ways. He or she might be the only person a farmer sees (outside of family) over a couple of days. Whether they chat for five minutes or longer, regular callers to farms are important. I noticed one farmer lament that his milk is now collected at night, which means he no longer gets to have a five-minute chat with the milk collector. It was only a few minutes but it was important social interaction to him. He probably realised he enjoyed it only when it ended.

So, the next time a sales rep annoys you, remember they fulfil other purposes too.

Don't buy a pig in a poke.

 Whenever you purchase something, check that you're getting what you paid for. Don't wait to get home before you check the bag, you might find it's something completely different to a pig in there.

THERE'S SOMETHING ABOUT MONEY

Some think money grows on trees when it comes to farming. Unfortunately, it can feel more like you're flushing it down the toilet at times.

Common situations:

⬛ You are asset rich but cash poor (the land is worth significant money but the return on investment is low).

⬛ It's a family farm and if you're in your twenties or early thirties and your parents are in their fifties, it can be a challenge for the farm to provide two incomes.

⬛ As well as requiring money for a salary (or salaries), the farm also needs finance for reinvestment and bank repayments.

⬛ Sometimes the son (even if in his 30s) may be getting much less than the minimum wage for his work; this presents difficulties when he wants to build a house with his partner and seek bank loans for farm improvements.

It's easy to feel the farm doesn't make any money if:

◢ A monthly salary isn't paid out from the farm into a personal account and you don't have a grasp on how much it actually costs to exist.

◢ The turnover is good but the profit isn't so hot.

◢ You're not paying yourself enough and have to dip into your "rainy day reserve" for living expenses.

◢ You can't save for a holiday.

◢ You aren't keeping tabs on cost control by keeping track of incomings and outgoings.

◢ There's no money left at the end of the year to pay the tax bill and the account goes deeper into the red. (Keeping the bank account in the black is a myth for most of us. Overdrafts are a fact of life in farming so don't lose any sleep over them, but it is important to feel you earn a reasonable salary from the farm.)

◢ Your wife's salary is paying the mortgage, household bills, childcare and family expenses. As the saying goes "behind every successful farmer is a wife who works in town".

Talk to your partner

It's important to include your partner in farm decisions especially when it involves spending money, because:

◢ Two heads are better than one.

◢ She is part of the business and its future.

◢ If you don't include her, she will wonder where all the money has gone.

◢ It might make you face up to calculating the cash flow for the year.

◢ If you spend money on a new tractor but can't afford a weekend away, she's not going to be happy unless she approved the tractor purchase – you might as well put your head on the guillotine right now.

◢ If you decide to expand and thereby invest heavily in the farm, and it can't afford to pay you a salary for a couple of years, you need her agreement as it will affect her too.

Never ask her to put her pension as collateral for a loan. If the farm goes, so does her pension.

You might think a new kitchen or a new bathroom is a waste of money as it won't create more income, but if she's still putting up with a 1980s kitchen in the old farmhouse and has accumulated three years' worth of kitchen magazines, I can assure you a new kitchen is a lot cheaper than a divorce.

How to get on well with your bank manager

A good relationship with your bank manager is essential. I'm not suggesting anything saucy but it helps if you get on well. You need to be able to pick up the phone and have a proper conversation with him or her if things go amiss financially.

The first thing is to establish if you're compatible. I know, it doesn't look promising on appearances. You wear checked shirts and jeans and he/she wears a pinstriped suit. Never fear, most managers try to find a common ground by assuring you they come from a farming background or spent summers at an uncle's farm so they know one end of a cow from the other. That first meeting can be a little like a first date when you're both trying to impress each other. It's only when things go awry that your relationship meets its first stumbling block. This is when you find out if you are going to get through thick and thin together.

Bank managers don't make many decisions now. They are now called "relationship managers" and it is their job to persuade us to be happy with the bank. They seem to be trying to obliterate the image of wolves in sheep's clothing! Decisions are made by "Credit", a mass of seemingly unfeeling robots who would be at home in Dickens' *Hard Times*. The managers can blame things on "Credit" yet have to convince us "Credit" is an unmovable block requiring the feeding of sacrificial humans on a regular basis. If we don't toe the line, we just might be the next sacrifices.

A wolf in sheep's clothing.

A person who appears friendly and helpful but is really hostile and perhaps dangerous.

Tips for applying for a loan

- ◢ Be confident: remember you are asset rich (albeit cash poor) and banks want to do business with farmers. The ball is in your court as long as you have a good track record.

- ◢ Bank managers may act like they are doing their best for you but remember their first loyalty is to the bank, so don't be swayed too easily.

- ◢ Have your business plan and repayment strategy in place. Be prepared to negotiate when it comes to margins and interest rates so do your homework beforehand.

- ◢ View it as a challenge for you and your wife to relish and enjoy. Both of you should go to the meeting: two heads are better than one when arguing!

- ◢ Check the small print as banks expect security and it's not unknown for the entirety of a farm to be used as security for relatively small loans.

⏶ Remember your bank manager is a gatekeeper so he/she can translate the message to Credit. I know Brian has, through infuriation, told me to tell the bank to f*** off when they were looking for more securities. On one occasion, my limits of subtlety having being exhausted, I simply translated it into "tell Credit they can go sing for it" and it worked.

⏶ Be firm and pick your battles. You won't win all of them but know the ones you want to win.

⏶ Above all, don't go with a bank that has a reputation for being aggressive if clients have difficulties making repayments. You never know what is around the corner.

How to maintain a good relationship with your bank manager

⏶ Respond to phone calls or emails.

⏶ Let them know if you're having problems making loan repayments.

⏶ Don't bother making jokes, they don't understand them.

⏶ Flag any future problems as soon as you're aware of them; for example, if you'll have problems paying the income tax in October.

⏶ Some people give their bank managers a bottle of whiskey at Christmas or a dozen eggs at each meeting. I might push the boat out occasionally and have biscuit cake available when he calls for a meeting.

We're on our sixth bank manager in 14 years. We're not killing them off: the bank keeps moving them around. The best ones are steady Eddies: straight talking, respectful, efficient and understanding. If they want to "link up", "hook up" or "touch base", watch out!

HOW TO STAY CALM

All too often, we end up behaving like a hen on a hot griddle because we're stressed. A farmer who shouts and stamps is not attractive, so if you need to let off steam, take yourself off to a distant field to do so. If you are the type to be annoyed easily, you'll end up having a heart attack as life never runs smooth when animals and the weather are involved.

Should you be practising mindfulness? Mindfulness? Go to a retreat together and hum or meditate or do yoga? Repeat inspiring quotes to oneself? Try not to think about all the work waiting when you get home? Fat chance.

Some of us get sufficient relaxation from hobbies, be they reading, cycling, gardening or playing football. Some of us love farming so much we work all the time and don't see anything wrong with that. However, it's sensible to take time to smell the roses (well, the honeysuckle and the freshly cut grass). That's where wives and children can come in handy: they make men slow down and appreciate the beauty in the ordinary. Take the time to admire the sunrise and the sunset with them and kick a football around the garden.

I find bringing in the cows, particularly if their journey home is along a scenic route such as our meandering lane filled with honeysuckle and blackberries in the summer and autumn, to be my most relaxing half hour of the day. The cows walk along so confidently and languidly there is no point in rushing them. I know lots of farmers use tractors or quads to bring in the cows, particularly if it's a distance to walk them home, but how can you relax on a quad? Get off the machine and stroll along, hand in hand with one of the children. You may even feel transported back in time to when your ancestors walked much the same route.

Like a hen on a hot griddle.

When someone is excited or agitated and won't sit still.

HOW TO DEAL WITH ISOLATION

Although farmers often didn't have good transport years ago, they weren't as isolated. There were more farmers living nearby as farms were smaller then. People went to local fairs, there were more local shops, people visited each other's houses at night or met at the crossroads. There were more people walking or cycling along the roads who would stop for a chat.

It's true that some people love being on their own. For many, solitude is one of the reasons they love to farm, with the peace and quiet of their own space in the yard and fields. For others though, days on end of scarcely seeing anyone around the place can be too much. Loneliness can eat away at a person's soul until they feel empty and hollow. That's why farmers' union groups, sales people, local farm stores and regular visits to the mart are so important.

Some people may say that talking to yourself is a sign of madness, but of course talking to animals is perfectly normal. They don't answer you back; they are usually agreeable, they will even nod in agreement and open their mouths as if they are smiling. I'm not so sure that it's a good idea to rely on just animals for company though. It's very easy to get stuck in a rut and get into the habit of not going out and then realising you haven't seen anyone outside family for days.

It's all very well to say join social groups – a discussion group, sports club, a Men's Shed – and many do, but what if you're too shy? While women are more inclined to go if they can go with a friend, men don't tend to ask a friend to go with them. The advantage of Twitter means that you can chat to other farmers at any time of the day or night.

If your wife is more of an extrovert than you and likes to go out with friends or to a group, don't hold her back or begrudge her for going. You really need to go along with her some evenings too so decide on things you can do separately and together.

Draw up a bucket list of things you would like to see or achieve. Keep it simple and short but try to do one thing a year. If you'd like to read more books, join a book club. If you'd like to learn how to give a speech, join your local Toastmasters. If you'd like to lose weight, join the local athletic club. If you'd like to visit a Texan ranch, start saving for a holiday.

HOW TO DEAL WITH SEXISM

Does sexism still exist? I'm afraid so.

Most women working on farms have been asked, at some time or another, "Is the boss around?" Being told "You're looking at her" or "There's the gate" has almost eliminated it here as it's a long time since I last heard it. Although Brian was recently told: "She may be the boss but you wear the trousers"!

What does it stem from? Well, as inheritance tended to be patrilineal, men inherited and were viewed as "the boss". Farming is still viewed as a male profession by many. It seems daft though as women have always worked on farms. However, there was a gender division with the work. Some tasks were viewed as more appropriate for women: milking cows, feeding young stock and working with poultry. Even though 40 chickens equalled one cow in value and egg production was a significant source of income, before the 1950s any male over 13 years of age would have been insulted by a request to work with poultry.[74]

Why did women work in the farmyard and men in the fields? Why the gender division? And was that sexist? Research (in America) suggests it wasn't sexist but a class issue because:

> nothing was more telling about the class status of a farm than where a woman did her work. Women who were required to assist their husbands with the

harvest in the fields were considered drudges, and by association their husbands were agricultural failures. Women who could turn their back on the fields served as evidence of their husband's success and superiority.[75]

In other words, if women were seen doing "men's work", the farming family had lowered its status.

Can this argument be applied to Ireland's past too? After all, most women didn't work outside the home (mostly due to the marriage bar) but earned "pin money" from egg and butter sales. That term suggests it was pocket money, not the significant sum that kept many families afloat. As men were the landowners and also viewed as the breadwinners, they were viewed as "the boss"; the person who decided what was bought and sold. There are still some men who won't do business with a woman.

While confident when dealing with any chauvinism I encounter in the yard, experiencing it in a different setting still catches me by surprise. When we experienced blatant sexism from a professional adviser last November, we were so startled we didn't react appropriately at all. We should have called an end to the meeting there and then, even if it would have embarrassed others present. But when it happens out of the blue, you find yourself wondering "Is this really happening?", particularly when the sexist behaviour is mostly non-verbal (the person ignored me for most of the meeting). I spent half the meeting trying to work out if he was being sexist or if his social skills were so poor he couldn't look a woman in the eye. To add insult to injury, while the invoice was made out to both of us, the accompanying letter was addressed to Brian with "Private and confidential" on it. When I shared my experience with others, it seems many women are still experiencing this attitude from men in all walks of life.

What you can do to combat sexism

Each of you work to your strengths. If your wife is better at paperwork than you and has taken that role in the business, she should have responsibility for all sales and purchases too.

If you experience a sexist attitude when you are with your wife, challenge the person on it. While your wife is equally capable of complaining, a sexist person won't take her seriously. Putting him down with sly comments doesn't get the message across – you need to spell it out in simple words and be prepared to walk out of there. If possible, inform a senior manager or the owner why they are losing your business. If enough of us do it, things will change for our daughters.

Make it clear to anyone who asks about the next generation of farmers in your family that your daughters are just as able and as entitled to inherit the farm as your sons.

Teach your daughters to do anything they want to on the farm, be it milk cows, shear sheep, drive tractors, drive loaders – whatever it is, don't hold them back.

If your farm is being featured in a farming newspaper or similar, describe your wife as your equal in the business. Point out that the farm isn't farmed by Joe Smith whose wife is in the background doing the paperwork, standing in the gaps, cooking meals, feeding calves, milking cows and starting up a diversification project as extra income. Emphasise it is a partnership and both names should be included in the first line of the article. While you may be the one going to the mart and to the discussion groups (and she will encourage you to do so as she knows you need the interaction), make it clear she is an equal not just a helpmeet.

What about sexism at the mart? It still happens women get a male family member to sell animals for them believing that they won't get as good a price from male buyers. Don't be condescending towards women or try to get one over on them either. Play fair and treat them with respect.

HOW TO APPRECIATE YOUR BEST FRIEND

Who is your best friend – apart from your wife, of course? The guy you go to the pub with? Your mates in the discussion group? No, your best friend – and your best investment – is your dog. Here's why:

- He's like a shadow, always there.

- He often knows better than you what work has to be done next. You'll wonder where he is and discover he's already waiting for you at the machine for the next job.

- You can talk to your dog and he will always agree with you.

- He doesn't cost you much money, and he certainly wouldn't appreciate a professional grooming. A quick hose will do the trick, thank you very much.

- He's never happier than when there's a busy day of work ahead.

- He will protect you to the best of his ability.

- He never resents you for telling him off.

- He's happy enough with whatever food you give him but the leftovers from a Sunday roast with lots of gravy is his favourite.

He probably has the same attitude as you: better to wear out than rust out, so let him enjoy his work for as long as possible by letting him semi-retire when he starts to slow down.

Every Ideal Farm Husband must have a good working dog in order to save his wife much angst and running.

HOW TO BE A HAPPY FARMER

An Ideal Farm Husband is always able to look on the bright side, to find the silver lining, to have the glass half full.

Farmers often want more money, more land, more sheep, heavier crops ... but would we be satisfied if we achieved that? Is it more about the journey than the destination? Admit it, if you were to get the farm to the stage where it didn't need any more improvements and everything was ticking along, if you just had to keep the wheels turning instead of looking for another challenge, would you be happy? Some would, but others would hate it.

Work out what makes you happy and strive to attain it. If it's about the challenge, then embrace it. Recognise as you attain each goal you'll still be setting up more until the day you die. Happiness isn't about obtaining everything you want, it's about appreciating what you have.

On a farm, happiness is ...

⬛ Sorting livestock together and knowing you'll still love each other when it's done.

⬛ Harvesting vegetables and fruits from your own garden.

◢ Seeing lambs gambol and calves caper in spring.

◢ Watching a sunrise with your wife.

◢ Taking a tractor ride together into the sunset.

◢ Splashing in huge puddles with the children.

◢ Having a water fight on a summer's evening.

◢ Seeing fields of golden corn.

◢ Seeing cows go out to grass for the first time each spring.

◢ Resuscitating a newborn calf and it breathing on its own.

◢ Giving thanks for your harvest.

◢ Leaning on a gate and watching the world go by (well, the birds and the animals).

◢ Smelling the heat of hot sun on hay and skin.

◢ Catching snowflakes on your tongue.

◢ Watching the grass grow.

◢ Seeing your children feed a lamb for the first time.

◢ Seeing a rainbow.

◢ Coming into a kitchen warmed by a woodburning stove on a freezing cold morning.

◢ Getting a good price for your livestock or crops.

◢ Eating eggs laid by your own hens.

◢ Seeing your young children out with their little buckets to pick blackberries, hunt for mushrooms or feed calves.

◢ Getting a clear tuberculosis test.

◢ Seeing your favourite cow have a heifer calf.

◢ Feeling rejuvenated by a walk across the hills in the wind.

◢ Counting the right number of cattle or sheep first time when herding.

◢ Coming home from a good family holiday and being keen to get back into work.

◢ Being able to work each and every day with your best friends (dog and wife!).

PART EIGHT

COMMUNITY LIVING

PILLAR OF THE COMMUNITY

Are you the type of person who gets involved in every farming, parish, school or sports organisation? Or are you very quiet, preferring to stay in the background? Do you make excuses yet send your long-suffering wife out to community things instead? Well, introvert or extrovert, farmers are involved in the community whether they like it or not. Our role affects others, both by what we do and what we don't do.

Road users

Whether pedestrians or drivers, neighbours or tourists, farmers provide them with:

Beautiful views

As people drive along, looking over ditches into fields or gazing into the distance at the patchwork of fields separated by tall green hedging or dry stone walls, they are admiring your work and that of your forebears. They see fields light green in spring, dotted with sheep and cows. Early June sees a patchwork of dark green, yellow green and brown fields as farmers start silage and slurry-spreading. Autumn brings the yellows of corn and the dark green of later grass, all separated by reddening foliage. The winter is beautiful too with dark branches of trees stark against the sky.

Hedges

Farmers always want to see over hedges into other farmers' fields. Everyone needs to see if cars are coming as they edge out on to narrow roads. Luckily, farmers are helpful creatures and cut the hedges. The hedgerows of farmers' fields provide the scent of honeysuckle in the summer too, not to mention providing nesting for lots of wildlife.

Vehicle recovery

Road accidents happen and cars end up in ditches. It's always a relief to hear that no one is hurt. Farmers are happy to help out and pull a car out of the ditch. Knights in shining armour on their diggers and tractors?

Excuses

Since farmers started pulling into the side of the road to let traffic past, we can no longer use with conviction the excuse "I was stuck behind a tractor for half an hour." Maybe we need to bring that one back so everyone has an excuse for being late. Brian used it 24 years ago as he was almost late for our wedding, getting there not long before me – apparently there were a lot of tractors bringing corn to Tullow.

Traffic jams

People move from the city to get away from smog and fumes and queues of traffic. They picture quiet country roads where they can cover ten miles in ten minutes. And then they meet you, and your sheep, not just crossing the road but walking along it for half a mile as you bring them from one field to another and they can't overtake.

Don't worry about rushing. After all, it is your duty to provide as much visual interest as possible so give the driver at least five minutes to take photographs and upload them to Snapchat, Instagram or Facebook with witty captions (such as "Traffic jam in XXX") so their friends can oooh and aaah. This also provides them with a valid excuse for being late. Have a dog out behind the sheep for the cute factor; you should look as traditional and as unshaven as possible so they can share photographs of the "stereotypical farmer". Don't forget to give them a big smile and a wave so they remain convinced of your friendly nature.

If they aren't of the "photo-taking" ilk and remain stoically sour-faced, your big friendly wave and smile will annoy them all the more. Should they happen to complain about having to wait for ten minutes, just reply with something like "Sure, I've been waiting all my life for someone like you to come along" and see them accelerate! Do take care to avoid times like school collections though or your life won't be worth living.

Farm "amenities"

Our fields are primarily used for feeding livestock and growing crops but can come in handy in other ways too.

Car parks

Even if you're not an usher, helper or on the C-list of mourners at a rural funeral, you still end up with a job. If your farm is near a church, one of the fields might be used as a car park. You'll be reeled in as a car park attendant as people from towns are never sure how to drive or park in a field and have to be beckoned into the designated spot.

Walking

There are public pathways through many farms in the UK, not so much here in Ireland, although whether there will be more cycle paths through some farms in the future remains to be seen. Farmers do let neighbours walk across their fields at times. We've seen neighbours exercising their dogs in fields on our out-farm and while we don't mind in principle, the reality is it can cause serious repercussions. The parasite Neospora, which is in dogs' excrement, can cause abortions in cattle and sheep when they ingest the parasite from the grass.

Dogs can also scare and injure livestock terribly. There seems to be numerous reports countrywide each year of sheep being attacked and killed by dogs. Bigger livestock can be affected too. Earlier this year, shortly after the yearling steers had been put out to grass, we found the 40 of them huddled in a far corner of their field, totally spooked. All we could do was leave them in peace and hope they'd venture out soon. By the evening, most were back grazing but one had disappeared. After two days of looking, we eventually spotted him in a neighbour's field; he had been hiding in an overgrown scrub patch in the middle of a corn field. Totally spooked, it took us four hours the next day to manage to get him back into one of the sheds. He lost condition and is still flighty and nervous.

We need to explain why we're not so welcoming sometimes: there are genuine concerns about dogs roaming or even being exercised under supervision in farmers' fields.

Farmyard manure

Does manure bring joy to anyone apart from the farmer? Neighbours probably don't want the smell of slurry too often. After all, we're not so keen either. It can be quite a contentious subject with occasional rural dwellers or visitors claiming that the spreading of such a substance is an outrage and making official complaints. It has to be spread though, and naturally enough farmers are going to do so when weather conditions are right and when it can be of optimum benefit to the crop. Sometimes a text message the night before can be a good idea just in case they have a week's washing out on the line. Most rural dwellers know though, once the silage is in, the smell will follow.

However, some neighbours will be glad of manure. Whether they are smallholders or just growing some vegetables and rhubarb, they'll appreciate some well-rotted farmyard manure. One of my granduncles used to take home bags of the stuff every year for his allotment!

Entertainment

Can farmers provide entertainment? Of course we do. Haven't you noticed the increase in "farm reality" TV shows recently?

Late night revelry

No, I don't mean farmers have raves – well, not too many of them do. No, you keep the neighbours awake with the contractors bringing your silage home from various fields until 2am, driving trundling tractors and trailers with flashing orange beacons along the road and by their houses. You hope it will lull them to sleep but it doesn't always work out that way. When I enquired on Twitter though, it seems most rural dwellers enjoy the spectacle of seeing the fields empty of cut grass, their children enjoy watching the machinery going to and fro and even the adults feel part of it, wondering if it will be finished before the rain comes. It seems to bring a sense of nostalgia as well as an appreciation of the cycles of the seasons.

Tractor rides and dinners

Neighbouring teenage children often wander down to silage fields to get a ride on one of the contractor's tractors.

Sometimes they get a meal from the farmer's wife too. Once I gave a lad a dinner without knowing who he was. The contractors had come in for dinner and left him on a tractor to wait. My dad spotted him and invited him in. I didn't pay any heed as the two of them took the last places at the table and I served them dinner. I did notice he seemed more appreciative than most, especially when I handed him a dessert. There was no sign of him at teatime and as I was missing signs of appreciation, I asked the others where he was. No one seemed to know even *who* he was. It turned out he lived about a mile away from our out-farm and had walked down for a spin on a tractor for an afternoon's entertainment. Some try to earn the meal by staying to cover the silage pit too. I can never tell them apart anyway – I could be serving up dinner to anyone!

Fundraising and educational events

Farmers take part in lots of fundraising events, many of which also educate and inform people about farming. During the summer, there are always tractor runs, threshings, steam rallies, heritage events and agricultural shows on around the country. Most agricultural shows have a vintage element, where cars and tractors are on display with owners nearby happy to answer questions. While the #Farm1916 event wasn't fundraising, entrance was free and hundreds of people volunteered to help Teagasc in the organising of it.

Farmers are also extremely generous in giving to charities, both local and abroad. Apart from financial donations, they donate farm products to auctions, do tractor runs for charity, help to organise field days and threshings, and either donate money or supply animals to go to people abroad.

Sex outdoors

I'm not suggesting your neighbours are turning into voyeurs or that you're getting frisky among the hay bales (but if that's your thing, work away). However, as we know, but some people tend to be surprised by, animals have sex. In public. In the middle of the field in full view of anyone who is passing. No shame. No embarrassment. It happens that farmers receive requests to move such animals because the neighbour's child has a birthday party the next day and there are 30 eight-year-olds coming. It also happens that visitors to a child's birthday party get the facts of life lesson from the farmer's child.

Country conversations

We forget we can look a bit scary or intimidating. We're often unshaven (that's the men!), our clothes can be a tad unkempt and we speak in gruff tones occasionally. Those originally from the city might be a little cautious, after all, they don't understand half of the lingo but they are keen to make conversation. They might ask how the calving is going and we'll start talking about "springers" and whether one is "humouring" and how one calved but didn't have much "beestings".[76] All they can do is smile and go away thinking you have a cow doing a comedy slot on a trampoline, which narrowly escaped being stung. That should keep them pondering for the rest of the day.

And yes, we Irish manage to regale each other quite effortlessly for at least ten minutes discussing what the weather has done for the last three days, what it is like today and what the forecast is likely to be for the next week. After all, it changes on a daily, if not hourly, basis.

COMMUNITY LIVING

Love it or hate it, you have to get involved to some extent. Sometimes the politics are too great to warrant the hassle of being on a committee and if you're naturally shy, you'd probably hate it anyway. However, you can't expect your poor wife to do double unless she's a natural organiser and extrovert. You have to make a bit of an effort but you probably do so without even realising it. If you help neighbours when there's a bereavement, work as a parking attendant at a fundraising event, pop in to see elderly neighbours or cut the grass in the graveyard, you're helping your community. So stand proud!

Good neighbours

Farmers tend to be good neighbours. There's always one of course, who gives the rest of us a bad name. However, you could argue the rest of us are appreciated more if there's one bad egg. To be good neighbours, we must:

- Maintain good fences.
- Stand in a gap when we come across others moving livestock.

- Be willing to lend machinery that isn't used that frequently. You might have a bale trailer and a neighbour has a big cattle trailer. It makes sense if you both borrow and lend.

- Offer support at times of bereavement by offering to do some farm work and provide refreshments to mourners and visitors.

- Pull any ragwort! It can easily spread to other fields.

- Look in on those who might be isolated in bad weather or lonely at any time.

Farmers need neighbours to be helpful. We need them to let us know if cattle or sheep have got out. We need them to stand in a gap on occasion or shut their garden gate so the marauding animals don't get in. We need them to stop their car and wait patiently while we move livestock across the road. We need them to tolerate the noise of machinery as we work to get the last of the silage or corn harvested before rain comes in.

We're extremely lucky as most of our neighbours are either farmers or have lived in this rural area for years and know what to expect in terms of farmyard noises, smells and yes, the occasional cattle breakout. On St Patrick's Day this year, I decided to treat myself to a lie-on but on hearing a knock on the front door at 7:30 I guessed something was up. The cattle we had put into a field on our out-farm two days previously were "everywhere, all over the road". On the way to check it out, we got a text from another neighbour. We drove past the field and discovered the cattle had got out because someone had stolen the gate – the only newish gate on the whole farm over there. Yes, our jaws dropped open. Luckily the heifers hadn't gone far and were standing huddled further up the road with another neighbour there ready to give us a hand to get them back in.

No damage done despite the thieves, but it was thanks to three good neighbours.

COUNTRY LIVING

Is country living all sweetness and light, pretty florals and community fetes?

Goldfish bowl

Country living means everyone knows exactly what everyone is doing. Even if your neighbours have high electric gates, you can get a good view from the height of your tractor. The smallest of things stimulates gossip in the countryside: from who got the silage cut first to who must be trying to lose weight judging by the amount of walking they are doing.

Mind you, don't think that comings and goings are of interest only to country neighbours. When Brian and I were renovating a townhouse (pre-farming days), it was so hot the week we moved in that we tackled the shed in the garden first. We discovered later that the neighbours were all talking about its new green walls and red roof, and wondering what sort of people would tackle the shed first.

The thing is, rural gossip is rarely malicious – well, not very. Its main function is to make country life more entertaining and interesting. On a slow day, it will focus on the weather and a new paint colour on someone's door. Normally, it will be stories of suspected affairs, marriage break-ups, bizarre wills with a distant relative inheriting a farm, or thefts from farmyards. Of course, when you first get married or start living with your partner, she will be the centre of attention for at least six months. You may have to shield her from the worst of it by laughing it off or doing things deliberately to create some gossip. Getting yourself featured in a newspaper might be the most effective method.

PART NINE

DOING YOUR BIT FOR AGRICULTURE

HOW TO ADVOCATE

Why is it important that farmers themselves become advocates for agriculture? I mentioned earlier how the media influences how farmers are perceived by the creation of stereotypes. As consumers become further removed from farming, much of the population doesn't have any contact with farmers and hence might believe inaccurate stories that will affect how we, and the food they eat, are represented.

We need to bear the following in mind:

◢ Do we really want to be stereotyped as hillbillies again – or worse?

◢ Photographs of some farming practices are being edited to show them in a negative light.

◢ Consumers are being further removed from farming and the disconnect between urban and rural dwellers is increasing. They just don't know how the other half lives. Less than 1% of America's population and 2% of Canada's population now farms. In Ireland, many people of our generation, if not brought up on a farm, visited farming cousins or grandparents, but that's fading fast with the next generation. Many urban people don't know any farmers so they don't know who to believe.

⬛ We assume people know there can't be antibiotics in their milk, their cheese and their meat because we're so aware of the stringent tests to ensure that all farmers adhere to the withdrawal periods, but consumers aren't aware at all. They see scaremongering stories about antibiotics or, perhaps worse, see some food advertised as "antibiotic-free" and wonder if the rest has antibiotics. We have to show that we hold ourselves to account. We have to dispel those misconceptions.

⬛ We need to show people our own farming practices. More and more farmhouses are offering Airbnb accommodation and visitors can visit the farm. But we can also share photographs and stories online.

⬛ Apparently, we trust only an average of 14% of advertisements, but 90% of us trust recommendations from our friends and people we know. It doesn't mean that we have to take time out from the farm to educate people; they can get to know us via our blogs and social media platforms.

⬛ We should be sharing our farming stories, sharing the tears when things don't go to plan but also sharing our pride and happiness when they go well.

In short, we need to share our own stories before others do. We need to show our pride in farming. Even if you don't supply a product directly to market (e.g. your own branded butter, your own yoghurts or your own turkeys) you are still representing your own type of farming in your country.

The Australian rural lobby group "AgForce" is hiring popular "stay at home mum" Jody Allen[77] to tell her enormous and largely female following about their farming methods and how food is produced. It's important to remember women make most of the spending decisions in a household. Consumers don't necessarily want to hear from "experts", politicians or celebrities about how food is produced. They want to hear it from the "horse's mouth" and Jody shares her experiences of visiting farms on her very popular blog.

Some UK dairy farmers campaign for processors to sell milk as "free range milk" in order to get a price that's sustainable and to reassure consumers of their farming practices.[78] Ireland has long had a reputation for grass fed and green products but perhaps we should be making more of it. Perception is reality and how people see farmers will affect the respect they have for us and the price they are willing to pay for our products.

How to "agvocate" - what methods will you use?

As food producers, we have to take responsibility for how farmers are represented. We have to "agvocate" for agriculture, to educate, and to support each other. We'll all choose different ways and that's fine. Is this book an example of advocating? Yes it is. Even if 99% of its readers are farmers, the 1% that aren't plus all those people who hear me talking on the radio or read about the book in newspapers will know that bit more about farmers' lives.

We also have to take responsibility for educating people. Farmers are accused of all kinds of cruel acts from raping cows to murdering livestock. However, hitting back with insults or profanity won't help. Remember, most people have never stepped on to a farm. Showing them how you, as "an ideal farmer", farm might get one or two or three more people on our side.

Choose your method for advocating

Photographs

Using smartphones makes it so much easier to take and share photographs. Even just sharing photographs of young calves in large airy sheds with straw bedding shows they are well looked after; photographs of your hens outside proves that they are free range; photographs of bringing the cows home to be milked confirms they too are "free range". It's then a case of sharing those photographs on your social media channels. If your wife is a better photographer, she could take on that enjoyable task.

Some professional photographers have taken it a step further: Ciara Ryan has created the Irish Farmer Calendar: a fun look at Irish farmers; Suzanna Crampton has increased awareness of female farmers and Zwartbles sheep, mostly through her Twitter and Vine accounts; and Audra Mulkern's Female Farmer Project shares photographs of ordinary farming women doing ordinary jobs on the farm in order to document the rise of women in agriculture.[79]

Video

Farmers are taking to YouTube to share videos of their farms. The most famous example has to be the Peterson brothers with their "I'm Farming and I Grow It" parody song. Simple videos uploaded to Snapchat, Vine or YouTube showing people how you farm will get the message out there. It's fun too.

Open farms/farmhouse holidays

By opening our farms to the public, particularly through educational days like Open Farm Sundays, those who have never been on a farm or have no contact with farmers, get an insight into what farming life is like.

Social media

Social media is another effective method of advocating. It's hugely enjoyable too, and the next section explains how to do it.

SOCIAL MEDIA

How to use Twitter

What is a tweet? A tweet is a message up to 140 characters long. People follow others so they can see their tweets in their news feed. They use it to chat about all kinds of things – how their day is going, to catch up on national and international news events, to share photographs, to ask questions, to discuss issues, to chat about sport. You can send private tweets (direct messages) on Twitter but tweets themselves are public.

You can have conversations with one or more people by sending them a tweet. Their username is prefixed by the @ symbol, so if you wanted to send me a tweet (please do and say hello), just include @IrishFarmerette within the tweet; I will see it, reply and follow you back. Another person's tweet that includes your username shows up in your 'notifications' tab so you don't miss it.

How do I get started?

Go to www.twitter.com and follow the instructions. You will need a photograph of yourself (400 × 400 pixels) to use as an avatar and a wide 1500 × 500 image for your header photo. To edit and resize photographs, use canva.com or picmonkey.com. You'll need to decide on a username too. Many people use their own name and if it's not available, add numbers, e.g. @JohnSmith65.

How do I find people to follow?

Twitter will suggest people to you, based on the interests you indicate, but the easiest way is to go to one farmer's account (you could do this with mine) and click on the "Following" or "Followers" button under their header image. You can then follow any of those tweeps.

Why do farmers use Twitter?

Farmers seem to love Twitter. They dip in and out as time allows and they're definitely on it more in the evenings. Many ask questions and describe it as a discussion group in their pocket. They use it to educate consumers, share photographs of their farm and get to know other people. Irish farmers definitely use it for banter too – a lot of teasing goes on!

How often should I tweet?

As frequently or as infrequently as you want.

What should I tweet about?

Share photographs from your farm, ask and answer questions, say hello. If you feel shy or nervous, follow others for a while to get a feel for how it works before you send your own messages.

Top tip

Never tweet anything you would mind seeing on the front of a newspaper.

What if someone is aggressive towards me; what do I do?

This is rare but you can block people should you need to. You can also report them to Twitter. Since I started using Twitter in 2009, I think I've blocked one person so it's not endemic.

How to use Snapchat

What is Snapchat?

Snapchat is a hugely popular mobile messaging app. Users send photographs and videos to each other or display them to followers. It is also used for sending and receiving text messages. Users create stories with multiple photos or 10-second videos – for example, showing how to cook a meal or how progress is going with the building of a shed. The photos and videos disappear after 24 hours.

How do I set it up?

Download the app and follow the instructions.

How do I find people to follow?

Sometimes other snapchatters recommend people or users share their Snapchat profile on other social media channels. It also shows you which of your contacts are on Snapchat.

What makes it fun?

The prevalence of reality TV programmes demonstrates most of us love seeing snippets from people's lives and Snapchat provides that. It also has lots of fun features where you can add special effects, text, line drawings and more to your photos and videos.

What kind of content should I share?

Like the other platforms, material from the farm and your life that you think others will find interesting. Snapchat videos go viral occasionally, by the way, so if you happen to share a video of your wife getting splattered with dung or something similar, make sure you have her permission first!

How to use Instagram

What is Instagram?

Instagram is a mobile app which allows you to share photographs and videos with your friends and followers.

How do I set it up?

Once you've downloaded the app, it's a case of following the instructions. You'll need a username, a photo to use as your avatar and a bio. You can share photographs from your camera or take photos and videos within the app. Instagram offers lots of different filters to make your photographs even more striking. You can also share "stories" there too, for example, creating a "story" showing getting animals in to be dosed, how they are dosed, clipping their tails and letting them out again. If something funny happens in the middle of it all, all the better.

What kind of photographs and videos should I share?

Almost anything goes but beautiful landscapes, fabulous flowers, cute animals and of course, scrumptious cakes, will be the most popular. Once you have added a filter to your photographs, write a caption and add some hashtags. People search for relevant content on Instagram using hashtags so this will help your photographs reach more viewers.

How do I find people to follow?

By tapping the search icon (the little magnifying glass) you can search for people by name and username, or your friends on Facebook will be flagged as suggested people to follow. You can also search for relevant people to follow by searching for hashtags used on photographs. Common farming hashtags include #farm365 #farminglife #farmerswife #farmlife and of course #perfectfarmwife and #idealfarmhusband.

How often should I post?

It really doesn't matter; it's more about the quality than the quantity although it can be annoying to see six photographs in a row from the same person if the content is very similar.

How to use Facebook

If you're using Facebook on a personal basis already, you'll have set up a "profile" using your own name. You're using it to connect with friends and catch up on news.

In order to use Facebook to advocate, you should set up a Facebook page, calling it the name of your farm perhaps, and people have to "like" it to see your updates in their newsfeed.

How do I set it up?

Go to www.facebook.com/pages/create and follow the steps. You'll need photographs for your avatar and your cover image.

What do I put on my Facebook page?

Share photos and videos and updates of what is happening on your farm. You can use it to discuss issues, although you always have to be careful of how others will interpret what you say. If you share a photo of an animal in a wheelbarrow or a crate for example, the vast majority of the population know you're using it to move a young animal from one shed to another, because as we all know, newborn calves aren't always the easiest to move along. However, there are those who will use that photo to 'prove' that animals are caged within crates so be careful. Don't let that put you off; just be mindful of how things can be interpreted incorrectly.

Starting a blog

What is a blog?

A blog can be described as an online diary. You write entries whenever you wish and your most recent blog post is the first one people can view as they are stored in reverse chronological order.

Why do people read farming blogs?

Reading blogs is a great way to get to know other farmers as well as finding out about different ways of farming. Consumers read them too. People have a genuine interest to learn about farming and find out how their food is produced. They often need a detailed explanation with lots of photographs to get an appreciation for the work as well as the beauty of what we do. If you speak frankly, consumers will believe and trust you.

What will I get out of it?

That depends on your personality and your enjoyment of writing – it can certainly be cathartic. You'll get to know more people, both online and offline, because of your blog. Your communication should improve as you become more familiar with the type of questions people ask.

If you are selling a product directly to market, a blog is an important part of your marketing strategy. You never know where it might lead. My first book was inspired by the first of my blog posts to go viral. If you have dreams of writing a book, a blog is a good way to start.

Where do I start?

You can start on a free platform such as wordpress.com or blogspot.com. By searching for instructions, it's fairly easy to get started. Many farmers give their blog the farm name or their own name. You'll need a couple of photographs and an idea for your first blog post. Don't be too focused on making it perfect. I'm sure I'd cringe if I looked back at my first blog post. The most important thing is to introduce yourself and your farm and hit the 'publish' button. You can find other farming blogs by searching for "farm blog" on a search engine or within Wordpress or BlogSpot. Mine is at www.LornaSixsmith.com.

Ideas for blog posts

⊿ Answer questions – For example, "Are there antibiotics in the milk we drink?"

⊿ "My Farming Week" type posts – Tell people about your week, focusing on two or three of the most interesting, humorous or poignant things to have happened.

⊿ Recipes – Share your tried and tested recipes.

⊿ "Wordless Wednesday" or "Foto Friday" – Sometimes just one or two striking photographs with a minimum of text is all you need.

⊿ History – I've found that posts where I've shared stories about the history of our farm or about traditional methods of farming to be hugely popular.

⊿ Review posts – Review agricultural books, agricultural products or new labour-saving ideas.

⊿ Share expertise – Share your knowledge with others; "A Quick Guide to Keeping Chickens", "Ten Tips for Grass Management" or "How to Make Farmhouse Butter".

⊿ Interviews – Interview farmers (you can do this by email) or others working in agriculture.

⊿ Bust a myth – Tell people the truth about something.

By using social media platforms, others will get an insight into your farming practices. Not only does it educate, but it gives them confidence in the provenance of the food they are eating. Should any food scares arise, they know who to trust and who to ask, rather than perhaps believing news reports designed to inflame reaction.

It's also a wonderful way to get to know people. I have more friends now that I've met online first than offline. When I go to writing or farming events, I'm meeting people I know from Twitter or Instagram. Social media platforms provide a great introduction when you want to get to know people.

PART TEN

#IDEALFARMWIFE

MARRYING A FEMALE FARMER

Are there many female farmers?

Well, 12% of Ireland's farms are registered to women, although the number of women actively "in charge" will be less. Half of that 12% are over 65. It hasn't changed significantly since 1964 when an article reported that the percentage of female farmers changed from 13.5% in 1881 to 7.3% in 1951. Although the proportion of female farmers in Ireland was four times as many as in Denmark, there was concern that since many of them were over 65, they were considered "unlikely to be the people best qualified to exploit the nation's land".[80]

In America, 30% of those involved in farming are female but 14% are principal operators. In the UK, women are about 28% of the agricultural workforce and it seems female farmers are now at about 20% of the total with more and more women studying agriculture and food production at college.

It is important to realise that women aren't just farming. They seem to be more active in connecting with customers and educating them, not just about how to cook their products but also showing them the stories behind the farms and how the food is produced. They are effective advocates in agriculture, skilled in telling their stories and reaching their audiences.

The "Ladies in Beef" group in the UK works to increase support for beef by encouraging customers to buy and cook various cuts of beef. They work with supermarkets to promote beef, particularly for Great British Beef Week each year, and provide easy-to-follow recipes. The "Ladies in Pigs" group works to increase the awareness and consumption of Red Tractor pork, bacon, ham, gammon, and pork products like pork pies and sausages.

Therefore, the chances of marrying a female farmer are higher than you might expect.

Marrying a female farmer

Is it very different being a husband to a female farmer compared to a wife of a male farmer?

A female farmer works the same long hours as a male farmer and while her husband is more likely to be working off-farm than doing the childcare and paperwork, he still helps out in the evenings and at weekends. Farm husbands help by feeding calves, standing in gaps, making the dinner, sharing the housework, fetching and carrying and, of course, following instructions. They might call it "manure management" rather than spronging out dung but the job is the same thing.

Farmers' husbands seem to be very aware of the importance of pitching in and helping out, not because they feel their wives can't do it without them but because they recognise the challenges of working in a business on your own. They know that assistance, be it physical or just a listening ear, is always appreciated. They also know that living anywhere other than the farm isn't an option and they see the sense in that. When married to a farmer, male or female, it's nigh impossible to have a working life that's separate to the farm. Your life becomes entwined in the farm even if it's just standing in a gap or feeding a pet lamb before bedtime.

Do female farmers have to do things differently? Not much is the answer. Farming has become so mechanised now that the ability to be dextrous and skilled in managing machinery is more important than physical strength and, indeed, a woman who is farming for 10–14 hours a day might even be stronger and fitter with more knowledge of how to lift something than her office-working husband.

Pregnant women have milked cows up to their due date. Lambing sheep is really the only stumbling block when she is pregnant as there's the danger of miscarriage from possible infections passed during the birth of the lambs.

Are female farmers treated differently by other farmers? They may well be asked "Where's the boss?" once or twice but once they prove themselves by buying good stock at the mart, having good stock to sell or answering questions intelligently, male farmers seem to accept women as farmers and be non-judgemental from there on. I think there are so many male farmers who grew up in households where the woman was the real manager and who kept the show on the road, albeit from behind the scenes, they are just seeing what they knew all along – women are just as capable of running a farm.

Women in agriculture can feel isolated if they want to talk to someone who is in a similar situation. Another woman who knows what it's like when you have to work in the field all day without a loo nearby or head indoors after doing the milking and find you have to cook breakfast for yourself as there's no one else there. Maybe every farmer needs a wife! This is where connecting with other farm women is so important, be it in a group that meets regularly or online in a Facebook group.

Just as it's important for a male farmer to be congratulated on success and have family take the time to celebrate the achievements, even if it's just by something small like baking a cake or cracking open a couple of beers, female farmers need this support too. Everyone does really, no matter what their role in life.

Your role is the same as a farm wife's really. In both situations – as in all marriages – it is a partnership and you will work out between you the best way of working.

A farm husband needs to:

⌁ Be patient.

⌁ Help out at weekends.

⌁ Acknowledge that farming is part of their lives, 24/7.

⌁ Do some housework.

⌁ Stand in gaps.

⌁ Be supportive.

⌁ Be optimistic.

I think there's one huge advantage experienced by female farmers: their husbands don't seem to be as house-proud as wives so dropping corn all over the house, keeping newborn lambs in the kitchen or popping baby ducks in the bathtub isn't too much of a problem.

However, what about men who farm together with their wives, who marry into the farm and work with their father-in-law? If, as I would hope, more daughters inherit from their parents, this situation will become more common. He will have the challenge of being the "blow in", of all other farmers knowing exactly who he is but he doesn't know who they are and of them watching his every move.

Farming with a father-in-law will have similarities to farming with a father except maybe you might not be as quick to forgive each other after an argument. He will probably want to put his own stamp on the place, work as a team with his wife to ensure the business is a success and have goals he wants to achieve.

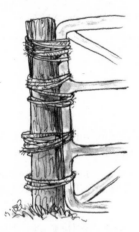

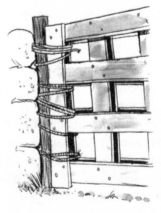

PART ELEVEN

SUCCESSION

SUCCESSION

Why is it that farm succession is so important to farming families?

Farming isn't just a business or a way of life. Farms are tied up in the history of generations past, grandparents and great grandparents who tilled the fields, milked cows and reared families, often through tough times. While land is sold once every 70 years or thereabouts in France, it changes hands only once every 400 years in Ireland such is the tie. For many families, they have farmed the same land for hundreds of years. They didn't sell up to increase scale by moving but purchased more land nearby. A farm could be in 3–5 different sections. Having the entire farm in one block, even if divided by a road, is not the norm in Ireland.

I'm the fourth generation to farm here. Garrendenny, our home farm, has been in Sixsmith ownership since 1904. It passed from my great granduncle Herbert Sixsmith to my grandfather George Sixsmith in 1946, to my father in 1964 and to me in 2003. Even though it's only four generations, there's still an immense tie to the place. I think, for most farmers, your land gets under your skin and becomes part of you, of who you are, and it can be as difficult to say goodbye to it as to a person.

WHO INHERITS?

How did parents decide which child would inherit the farm? Was it always the eldest? After the Great Famine, it became the norm that one son inherited the farm, usually the eldest. Other brothers emigrated, became priests or clergymen, worked on farms or in shops in local towns. Those who moved away were often treated like prodigal sons whenever they returned with gifts and new cars while the farmer's son got the job of killing the fattened calf and his wife had to cook the roast beef for all the visitors.

There seems to be a move away from giving the farm to the eldest towards trying to work out which child is most suited to farming. Of course, there's a sod's law element to this. Even with six children, it can happen that they all want it or none of them do. Frank discussions around the dinner table are required from when they are in their teens and making subject choices in school. Parents also need to plan financially for their own retirement.

The retiring couple, depending on their financial situation regarding their pension, may supplement their income by retaining some land and renting it to the younger couple or drawing up an agreement to receive a certain amount of money each year. Occasionally, they retain the whole farm in fear of a "gold-digging" wife running off with half of it if she divorces their son.

What happens when the father is too young to retire and the son is biting at his heels to take over? Partnerships are becoming popular where a legal agreement is drawn up for both parties. They also offer tax advantages. However, planning needs to be put in place to ensure two incomes can be derived from the farm, particularly for years when the product prices are low. If that's not possible, the son usually works elsewhere and helps out at weekends until the time comes when his father retires or needs more help. Many farmers have engineering, science or accountancy degrees as well as having qualifications in agriculture.

How do the non-inheriting siblings feel about it?

There can be jealousy that one child has been handed a valuable asset, particularly if they feel they didn't get much out of it. There often wasn't much cash to give to daughters and often a reluctance to spend money on her education if it was believed she was going to marry a farmer anyway. If a daughter gets very little from it and sees her brother inherit a farm that he then sells for millions a few years later, it's unlikely they would ever speak again. Yes, family feuds that started with jealousy over land can be quite common.

However, most siblings are now provided with a university education (so they get their livelihood just as the farmer does) and sometimes a site on which to build a house.

In Ireland, there's often relief when one child takes it over: the parents are happy and the land stays in the family name. The person inheriting is expected to pass it on to one of his or her children, to be a custodian, improve it and ensure it stays in the family.

It's quite different in America where rather than being given a farm (albeit often with debt or a promise to look after parents financially), the inheriting child pays the market value for the farm. The parents use this to fund their retirement and the non-farming children take their share, which can be a sizeable amount, e.g. $500,000 each.

What happens if no one wants to farm?

For generations, sons (and occasionally daughters) have followed in their father's footsteps. Not just in farming but in other occupations such as doctors, butchers, solicitors and shop owners. Times are changing though. There's more career choice; there's more acceptance of "difference" too. Just because a person is a doctor or a guard or a teacher, there's no reason his or her children should take the same route.

It can happen that none of the children want to farm and yet there is a reluctance to see the family farm sold. If the farm is small enough, i.e. 50 acres or less, the reason given is valid: it isn't big enough to sustain a family unless creating a niche product. The successor can work part-time or full-time and still keep a suckler herd or sheep. Siblings, even though they'd be materially better off if it were sold, are often relieved the farm will stay in the family.

For someone who doesn't want to farm but does it out of loyalty or little choice, the farm can be a poisoned chalice. A valuable asset yet perhaps not providing much income or enjoyment. Knowing that previous generations have managed to keep it during tough times means there's a fear of failure or guilt if it is sold. That fear of failure and shame is very real and farmers have committed suicide because of it. Yet, for those who decide to move on and apply their many skills to other jobs or businesses, they can flourish when the millstone is gone from around their neck.

Every situation is different but farming is now a profession requiring various skills as well as an optimistic outlook on life. Not everyone is suited to self-employment and there is no shame in that.

Why do parents hold on to the farm for so long?

Sometimes parents hold on to the farm for too long. Maybe they don't trust their child with it, perhaps they fear his wife will be a gold-digger, perhaps they want to retain control, perhaps they didn't get it early so don't see why a child should. There are serious ramifications to this: the person waiting to inherit will miss out on the advantages of being classed as a "young farmer" in terms of tax relief on increased stock numbers and financial assistance for improving the farm. Farming methods, and the consumption of different foods, are changing and farmers have to adapt to stay in business. Older farmers can sometimes be slow to change, which may not bode well for the future of the farm.

If the transfer is delayed, and the son is in the habit of doing what the father tells him to do, it's hard to suddenly change and make his own decisions. He may become sullen and resentful, feeling chained with no choice. His own time is limited in terms of making improvements on the farm as he will often need decades to make the repayments on loans, provide for his own pension and feel that the farm is in a good position to hand on.

Another reason parents hold on to it is if they don't consider daughters as successors if the sons aren't interested in farming.

Why do young people want to farm?

I think the days of an inheriting child not having any other choice are gone, at least for the majority of children. They are aware of the financial challenges, they are often well educated and love farming. They may have more staying power and more determination because they could make that choice to stay or go. They want to be self-employed. If they have experienced the "rat race", they may appreciate their workplace all the more: walks along meandering lanes, beautiful woodlands, grassy hills and shady glades and they see it as a wonderful place to live and rear a family.

Take the bull by the horns.

To confront the problem, or make a swift decision, certainly no dilly-dallying around.

HOW TO FARM WITH FAMILY WITHOUT KILLING EACH OTHER

If a son or daughter is waiting to inherit, there can be challenges. There is often a piggy in the middle who is the peacemaker (usually the mother/wife), stuck between a father and son who both want to farm in different ways, who may swear at each other when they are angry, stressed and frustrated; who both take it out on the peacemaker expecting her to take their side, and yet neither is right and neither is wrong. It's often just a generational thing, both seeing different ways of farming as the way it should be done. The young farmer is getting 'notions' from having been at college and seeing how things are done on other farms while the older farmer wants to continue doing things the way they have always been done and is perhaps a tad concerned about what the neighbours might say if the young lad carries out some of his mad ideas.

There may well be a honeymoon period. The parents will say "You can do what you want when you take over," but what it might really mean is "You can do what you want as long as you don't change anything." The inheriting child needs to have the confidence to apply best practice to the farm and ensure it stays profitable. They can't be like a puppet on a string. Ideally, the person inheriting should have worked abroad for a few years before coming home to farm; to experience other ways of farming, see good (and bad) working practice and working relationships, to know what it's like to be an employee in order to become a good employer. Too many young farmers in the past were worked too hard on family farms, were not treated with respect and maybe ended up feeling trapped. Maybe others got the farm too easily and never found out what hard work really was. By working elsewhere, they will see all types.

Mutual respect is hugely important. Many men (and women) retired from farming would die of boredom if they didn't get to visit the farm on a frequent, if not daily, basis. Very few farmers move away to the seaside or to sunny Spain upon retirement but stay within their community. Even if their strength and reaction wanes, they still visit to do a few jobs and find out what is going on.

Safety is as big an issue with older people as it is with children; in some ways it is more difficult because a child will do what they are told but an older person often thinks they know best and will be determined to do what they have always done. The reality is their reactions and reflexes will have slowed and unfortunately, statistics show that older people feature highly in farm deaths with animals.

Things your dad will say

He will have an opinion on everything. If you own the farm, you can do your own thing but if he still has the purse strings, it can be more difficult to make changes.

- "That'll never work." – Well, that will make you more determined to succeed.
- "What do you need that for?" – You'll hide the new purchase more carefully the next time.

◢ "Won't they do all right?" – Although phrased like a question, this is a statement and he doesn't want to spend money on replacing something.

◢ "What will that cost?" – He doesn't see the need to be extravagant.

◢ "That one paid a lot of bills." – When he doesn't want you to cull one of his old favourite cows even though her udder is nearly dragging on the ground and she keeps getting mastitis.

◢ "He's trying to do xxx but sure you can't put an old head on young shoulders. I may let him at it." – So if you do fail, all the neighbours know he didn't have anything to do with it.

◢ "I let him find out the hard way. I knew it wouldn't work but knew he wouldn't listen." – So he is off the hook and you look like a stubborn fool.

Things will happen that will make you despair sometimes. He will do things that end up creating more work for you. Something might go on fire and he'll think he can put it out rather than calling you and it ends up needing the fire brigade.

But you know he loves you dearly and he's proud of you. He might not admit it but he is. Remember too that while his workload will reduce as he gets older, he is still an important contributor to the family farm. His knowledge and expertise – for example, during a tricky calving – will be invaluable at times too. It's the simple things that often give him pleasure, from seeing calves and lambs born each year, seeing grandchildren bottle feeding the lambs, hearing of successes on the farm, that make you realise the farm is his life and it will be until the day he dies. When that does happen, an expression at the funeral will be 'His work is done' as people pay their respects and acknowledge his hard work over the decades in providing food and caring for the land.

YOUR WIFE'S ROLE ON THE FARM

Every situation is different but a daughter-in-law might not feel appreciated enough by the family for her efforts. Unfortunately, she's often damned if she does and damned if she doesn't.

If she takes an interest in the farm – she's seen as interfering.

If she doesn't take an interest in the farm – she's seen as not caring about it.

If she gets involved by milking cows and doing field work – she might be criticised for not bringing in an off-farm income.

If she works long hours off-farm – she might be criticised for not doing enough on the farm, why does she need a spa day on a Saturday anyway?

If she wants her husband to get in early to spend time with the kids – she's accused of being clingy and demanding and then she gets the blame if the relationship ends in a divorce.

The fact is, some farms wouldn't be able to sustain a family nowadays. Off-farm incomes are crucial to the future of many farms and often maintain the family when the farm is going through a period of expansion. A daughter-in-law needs to feel appreciated by her in-laws. Whether she is working off-farm, on the farm, or looking after small children, her role is important to the success of the family farm.

HOW TO ENCOURAGE CHILDREN TO FARM

Some children will love the farm from an early age and there will never be any question about their career choice. Others come back to it in their later years. Much of it is down to their personality but sometimes their upbringing and your actions can affect their outlook too. If you want them to farm, here's a few ideas for what you can do to encourage them to farm in the future:

- Let them see the pleasures in farming, the satisfaction of getting the harvest in, as well as the tough times when an animal dies.
- Celebrate the successes. The whole family should go out and celebrate occasionally. Make it special.
- Take time off to watch them play some matches, otherwise they may resent the farm if they see other dads there.
- Don't make them work all hours. Just because you chose a career where 18-hour days can be the norm at times doesn't mean they have to work long hours and rush doing their homework.

⏚ Never blame or humiliate them for things like not being able to stop an animal or forgetting to close a gate. Remember they'll choose your nursing home!

⏚ Some farmers have the expression "there's no money in farming" on repeat. If you are paying a mortgage, putting food on the tables, clothes on their backs and putting them through school and college, it is making money.

⏚ Build some fun into the farm week.

⏚ Let them go and experience life elsewhere. Let them do crazy things in their early twenties. Most of us settle down into reasonably normal human beings after that. Having those feelings quashed could mean they erupt as bizarre midlife crises in their forties.

⏚ Give them responsibilities when they are ready. If a teenager is really keen on farming, let them have their own enterprise. Buy them some sheep or cattle to get them started and let them run it as their own business. Most importantly, let them make mistakes and learn from them.

Go the whole hog.

You might as well finish it.

PART TWELVE

HOW TO RETIRE GRACEFULLY

RETIREMENT

> "Work is the best way of passing the time;
> better to wear out than rust out."

We're all living longer which is great news, but farming is one of those careers that it's not so easy to continue working in it full time once the body starts to slow down.

There's a saying that a farmer is a farmer until they are six feet under. However, the responsibility can become too much. Handing it over means that you can help out on the farm rather than being the decision-maker and having to worry about the risks of your actions.

It will take time to adjust. Your wife was accustomed to you being out on the farm all hours and now you're under her feet. While you can spend more time together, having days out and going on holidays, you probably don't want to live in each other's pockets either. If you feel too young to start wearing your slippers by the fire, you need something to keep you active and interested. Watch too much daytime television and your brain will turn to mush.

Retirement isn't about stopping work and waiting for God. It's about starting a new journey, taking things easier but enjoying the fruits of your labour. Many farmers will get more enjoyment from starting something new than heading to Spain to play golf.

Here are some ideas for businesses and voluntary work:

⌡ Ireland's farms tend to be fragmented into different holdings. If the farm has a holding with 20 acres and a couple of sheds, why not build your retirement home there. It means the new farming couple have some space too, you're not far away in case they need help or babysitting and you could keep a few cattle or even look after bull calves in quarantine for AI companies. After all, lots of office workers become small farmers on retirement.

⌡ Sell farm machinery.

⌡ Take on a role in the local farming group.

⌡ Work part-time recruiting members for the local farming group.

⌡ Help with teaching teenagers literacy skills.

⌡ Help at your local Men's Shed.

⌡ Woodwork – build things for sale.

⌡ Repair bicycles or motorbikes if you have a mechanical bent.

⌡ Start up a small pedigree herd of sheep or cattle.

⌡ Breed and train sheepdogs.

⌡ Start up a grass cutting or garden maintenance business.

⌡ Work part-time with a local contractor, when they need an extra person during busy times.

⌡ Grow vegetables in your garden for sale at the local farmers' market.

⌡ Keep bees.

⌡ Restore old tractors or old cars.

⌡ Get involved in local politics.

⌡ Take on a role at your local church – that could become nearly full-time if you want it to.

⌡ Become a guide at a local cathedral or stately home.

⌡ Join a local writers or historical group.

⌡ Help out on the farm and help to look after your grandkids.

QUIZ (FOR HIM)

1. A "happy dance" on the farm is when:
    (a) You get the Friday feeling that it's the weekend. Okay, you'll still be working over the weekend but reduced hours, and you know there'll be no sales reps calling. ❏
    (b) When the cows and younger cattle get to grass the first time each spring and caper around excitedly. ❏
    (c) Hmmm, it doesn't happen on our farm. ❏

2. There's a mouse in the house! Do you:
    (a) Set a couple of mouse traps and get rid of the offending animal when it's caught? ❏
    (b) Set the trap but hope it's caught and got rid of before you get in that evening as you're secretly terrified of them? ❏
    (c) Tell your wife not to be a wimp and let her deal with it? ❏

3. Your wife wants you to go to a school event with her, your mother wants help moving furniture today as visitors are coming, and the cattle need to be dosed. Do you:

(a) Ask your wife to help you with the cattle so you can go to the event together in the afternoon. Postpone your mum until tomorrow? ❏

(b) Manage to fit in all three and then collapse in a heap on the sofa at 11:30pm? ❏

(c) Dose the cattle? ❏

4. It's been a tough year financially as well as having to put in more hours than normal. It's time to consider whether you're going on holidays or not. Do you:

(a) Decide that if you're working that hard, you all deserve a good family holiday. You'll look at cheaper options this year but you'll still get away for a break? ❏

(b) Buy a tent and head for the weekend to Stony Sand Beach where it rains all weekend. The rain suited perfectly as otherwise you'd have been harvesting corn? ❏

(c) Suggest that your wife takes the children to her mother's for a week and you stay at home? ❏

5. You take the kids out on Sunday afternoon. Your wife is staying at home. Do you expect her to:

(a) Relax with a book, a cup of tea and a huge slice of cake? ❏

(b) Hoover a couple of rooms and go for a long walk? ❏

(c) Clean the house, prepare meals for next week and milk the cows? ❏

How did you do?

Mostly A's – Well done, you can now tell everyone you're an Ideal Farm Husband!

Mostly B's – You have great intentions but you plunge in sometimes without thinking.

Mostly C's – Admit it, you haven't read much of this book have you?

CONCLUSION

There's no doubt that a farming life is full of challenges and there will be days when you'll think an office job would be easier, but realistically those thoughts are few and far between. You will have bad days, that's a given. It might be because an animal died, or it rained just as you were about to harvest or you feel down in the dumps for no particular reason. That's normal and it's by experiencing the bad days that you'll really appreciate the good ones. Farming isn't just a job or an occupation, it's a lifestyle. It forms the structure and content of your life. It's often 24 hours a day for 6 days a week with a few hours off on a Sunday.

By deciding to become a farmer, you've embraced it and all it offers. Even on the days when it's lashing rain and the wind is blowing a gale, you can still appreciate that your occupation provides your own fields to walk across, peaceful meandering lanes, woodland paths, ancient trees, shady glades and hills from which to admire beautiful views. Compare that to working in an open plan office! You could consider that to be part of your annual salary.

Every now and then, Brian and I groan a little about the repayments we're making on land we purchased in 2006, but in my heart I know it was worth every cent because when I'm standing in one of those fields looking at the view that stretches out for miles, I feel on top of the world and yet incredibly peaceful.

You've read the book and now you know exactly what to do to fulfil the role of an Ideal Farm Husband. You can don the Superman cape now. Being an Ideal Farm Husband isn't about having the best bank balance or the newest tractor. It's about being resilient to setbacks and bad weather. It's about being optimistic and hoping next year will be better. It's about doing what you can to help a neighbour and putting your family first. It's about making your farming life a wonderful life experience for you, your wife and your children. And you've always done those – right?

It's also about being happy in your own skin; looking after yourself in terms of mind, body and spirit; caring for the environment and animal welfare; being able to laugh when the only other option is crying; enjoying the teamwork of being a family who farms together and taking the rough with the smooth.

I Now Pronounce You An <u>Ideal</u> Farm Husband.

FURTHER INFORMATION

Books

Irish farming history

A History of Irish Farming 1750–1950; *Rooted in the Soil* and *Irish Farming Life*, Jonathan Bell and Mervyn Watson

Agriculture and Settlement in Ireland, edited by Margaret Murphy and Matthew Stout

The Irish Countrywomen's Association, A History 1910–2000, Aileen Heverin

Farm memoirs

Breakfast The Night Before, Marjorie Quarton
A Year on Our Farm, Ann and Robin Talbot
The Lie of the Land, P. J. Cunningham
Around the Farm Gate, edited by P.J. Cunningham
Any Fool Can Be a Dairy Farmer, James Robertson
To School Through the Fields, Alice Taylor
The Yorkshire Shepherdess, Amanda Owen
Over the Farmer's Gate, Roger Evans
The Shepherd's Life, James Rebanks
The Days of the Servant Boy, Liam O'Donnell

The Farm by Lough Gur: the story of Mary Fogarty (Sissy
O'Brien), Mary Carbery
A Farm Daughter's Lament, Evelyn I Funda
Women Drive Tractors Too, edited by Mary Carroll

Twitter - curated farming accounts

A curated account is when a different person tweets from it for a
week, usually Monday to Sunday.
@IrelandsFarmers
@FarmersoftheUK
@FarmsoftheWorld
@AgoftheWorld
@SmallholderIrl
@FarmersofCanada
@SmallholdersUK

And I am going to mention two Irish Instagram accounts as
their photographs are amazing and will make you smile:
@brian.joyce
@siochanta_333

Please note that I haven't had personal experience of any of the
organisations listed below so am unable to give personal
recommendations or opinions on them.

Organisations that help with depression/stress

www.samaritans.org 116 123
www.aware.ie 1800 80 4848
www.grow.ie 1890 474 474
www.pieta.ie 1800 247 247

Dating/matchmaking websites

www.muddymatches.co.uk (UK and Ireland) – designed to
   bring together those who love the countryside
www.farmersonly.com (USA)
www.ozcountrysingles.com.au (Australia)
www.knockmarriageintroductions.com (Ireland)
www.twoscompany.ie (Ireland)

Some Infertility/miscarriage services in Ireland

www.miscarriage.ie
www.feileacain.ie – stillbirth and neonatal death
www.sims.ie
www.rotundaivf.ie
www.repromed.ie

NOTES

1 *Nenagh Guardian* 17 April 1965

2 *Irish Press* 9 October 1990

3 Apollo was an important god in Greek mythology. Michael Dwyer was a United Irishmen leader in the 1798 rebellion and went on to fight a guerrilla campaign against the British Army in the Wicklow Mountains from 1798 to 1803. To be Machiavellian is to act with subtle cunning. Robert Emmet was an Irish nationalist and Republican, an orator and rebel leader. He led an abortive rebellion against British rule in 1803 and was later hanged, drawn and quartered. The reference to Job is a biblical one and refers to endurance as well as patience.

4 *The Irish Press*, 10 January 1968

5 *Sunday Independent*, 16 April 1989

6 According to the census of 1946, just 8.6 per cent of rural homes had water on tap; in towns, which had benefited from state investment, the figure was 92 per cent.

7 http://thedublinreview.com/article/irelands-looming-water-crisis/

8 Heverin, Aileen, *The Irish Countrywomen's Association, A History 1910–2000* (Wolfhound Press, 2000), p112

9 Heverin, p112

10 *Nenagh Guardian*, 17 April 1965

11 The Irish Taoiseach is equivalent to the Prime Minister or President in other countries. It is pronounced "Tee-shock".

12 Bell, Jonathan and Watson, Mervyn, *Rooted in the Soil: A history of cottage gardens and allotments in Ireland since 1750* (Four Courts Press, 2012), p30

13 Maura Laverty's Letters page, 31 August 1963, quoted in Meehan, Ciara "How to Attract a Husband and be a Good Wife – 1960s style", 20 September 2014, www.ciarameehan.com

14 Letters to the Editor, *Woman's Way*, 1 June 1963, quoted in Meehan, Ciara "How to Attract a Husband and be a Good Wife – 1960s style", 20 September 2014, www.ciarameehan.com

15 A wellington boot can leave an indentation on the legs if worn often and for long durations, hence symbolising a farmer who works hard.

16 Arbuckle, John and Andrew, *Farming is a Funny Business* (Polaris Publishing, 2015), p74

17 *Irish Examiner*, 20 December 1955

18 *Longford Leader*, 26 May 1978

19 *Irish Examiner*, 25 October 1969

20 *Irish Independent*, 3 February 1937

21 *Irish Examiner*, 27 January 1955

22 *Western People*, 13 November 1991

23 MacDonagh, Michael, "Marriage customs in rural Ireland", *The Englishwoman*, 22 (April–June 1914)

24 *Western People*, 16 February 2008

25 *Irish Independent*, 3 February 1937

26 *Woman's Way*, May 1966, cited in Meehan, Ciara, 14 May 2015, www.ciarameehan.com

27 *Women's Choice*, 25 March 1969 cited in Meehan, Ciara, "Selling to women through 1960s magazine advertorials", 8 June 2016, www.ciarameehan.com

28 *Mayo News*, 2 January 1960

29 *Irish Press*, 10 January 1969

30 *Irish Farmers Journal*, 12 February 1966

31 *Irish Press*, 10 January 1969

32 *Nenagh Guardian*, 29 January 1921

33 *Irish Independent*, 13 October 2012

34 Morton, H. V., *In Search of Ireland* (Metheun, 1930, this edition, 1984), p199

35 *Irish Press*, 19 April 1973

36 Morton, p199

37 Carbery, Mary, *The Farm by Lough Gur: the story of Mary Fogarty* (Sissy O'Brien) (Longmans, Green and Co, 1937), p47

38 Bell, Jonathan and Watson, Mervyn, *Irish Farming Life: History and heritage*, (Four Courts Press, 2014), p25

39 Carbery, p259

40 *The Kerryman*, 16 November 1963

41 Bell and Watson, p26

42 *Irish Examiner*, 6 August 1994

43 Bracken aired on RTE from 1978 to 1982.

44 Ryan, Ciara, Irish Farmer Calendar, produced each November for the following year.

45 Evelyn Funda "Farming is the New Sexy" TEDxUSU talk on YouTube.

46 "Beef: 'Trophy husband' material and hobby farming – is this the future for beef men?", in *Irish Independent*, 13 July 2016

47 *Farmers Weekly* 9 October 2015, http://www.fwi.co.uk/farm-life/marriage-proposal-cultivated-in-field.htm

48 Agriland.ie 21 July 2015 http://www.agriland.ie/farming-news/crop-marks-for-farmers-marriage-proposal-with-a-difference/#

49 ABC News, 4 December 2015, http://www.abc.net.au/news/2015-12-04/marriage-proposal-bushfire-paddock-hay-bales/7000530

50 *Derby Telegraph*, 18 August 2015 http://www.derbytelegraph.co.uk/surprise-proposal-moo-sic-farmer-jo-sears/story-27624491-detail/story.html

51 ITV.com 24 August 2016 "Boyfriend proposes after farmers mow will you marry me"

52 Chronicle Live 5 October 2015 http://www.chroniclelive.co.uk/news/north-east-news/northumberland-farmer-andrew-gallon-ploughs-9902735

53 *Irish Press*, 27 February 1932

54 *Irish Press*, 6 May 1953

55 *Irish Independent*, 26 April 2016

56 Murphy, Theresa "Trust can resolve inheritance issues", *Farming Independent*, 2 August 2016

57 *Irish Independent*, 23 January 2012

58 *Irish Farmers Journal*, 23 July 2016

59 Articles by Catriona Murphy in the *Irish Independent* on 21 January 2012, 23 January 2012 and 24 January 2012

60 *The Good Life* was a very popular television programme on BBC in the 1970s. Tom Good left his city job and he and his wife Barbara led the good life in their suburban semi-detached house and garden with many humorous results.

61 Wrap It Pink is an initiative to raise funds for the Irish Cancer Society with Dairygold providing pink wrap and donating money from

sales. Pink bales around the countryside brighten it up too. Read more about it at www.cancer.ie/about-us/news/wrap-it-pink-back-for-2016

62 *Irish Times*, 5 November 2011

63 7Up (similar to Sprite) if allowed to go flat was reputed to cure all kinds of things from upset tummies to common colds. Our children always preferred it fizzy and yes, a day on the sofa always meant a bottle of 7Up was purchased from the local shop.

64 Data from Kantar Worldpanel indicates that almost half of dishes (in the UK) are now bought pre-prepared instead of being made from scratch. Source: http://beefandlamb.ahdb.org.uk/market-intelligence-news/2016-year-far-meat/

65 Bord Bia survey results from a "Cookery Confessional Poll" in *Woman's Way*, 27 July 2016. 2,025 people were interviewed in the UK and 400 in Ireland

66 Daly, Willie, *The Last Matchmaker* (Sphere, 2010), p128

67 *Sunday Independent*, 19 November 1944

68 *Sunday Independent*, 19 November 1944

69 Morton, p 114

70 A meitheal is a gathering of neighbours at one of the local farms to help with a task, for example, at harvest time. Neighbours moved from farm to farm, helping each other until everyone was finished.

71 O'Donnell, Liam, *The Days of the Servant Boy* (Mercier Press, 1997), p19

72 Carbery, Mary, The Farm by Lough Gur (London, 1937) in Luddy, Maria, *Women in Ireland 1800–1918* (Cork University Press, 1995), p172

73 Street, A.G., *Farmer's Glory* (Faber and Faber, 1932)

74 Bell & Watson p42

75 Funda, Evelyn I, *Weeds: A Farm Daughter's Lament* (University of Nebraska Press, 2013), p34–35

76 A springer refers to a cow that is going to calve soon; when her udder starts to fill with milk, she is described as "springing down". The term "freshen" is used in the US. "Humouring" means she is soon going to calve; she's showing some of the signs such as her udder has filled and her "pins" (bones either side of the tail) have dropped and perhaps she has isolated herself from the others and is "nesting". "Beestings" is a colloquial term for the colostrum.

77 www.stayathomemum.com.au

78 Neil Darwent of Free Range Dairy is one of the farmers behind the "pasture promise" initiative whereby farmers are paid a premium for their cows grazing grass outdoors for a minimum of 180 days a year.

79 Ryan, Ciara, Irish Farmers Calendar; Crampton, Suzanna on Twitter at @ZwartblesIE and Mulkern, Audra Mulkern at www.audramulkern.com

80 *Irish Farmers Journal*, 29 August 1964